W9-AZY-554

Historic
FIRES
of the West

by

RALPH W. ANDREWS

VIRGINIA M. TUTT BRANCH
2002 Miami Street
WITHDRAWN

TANGLE OF HOSES not enough to keep spectators back from burning Grand Trunk Dock— Seattle, July 30, 1914.

Bonanza Books • New York

COPYRIGHT © MCMLXVI BY SUPERIOR PUBLISHING COMPANY, SEATTLE, WASHINGTON

All Rights Reserved

This edition published by Bonanza Books,
a division of Crown Publishers, Inc.
by arrangement with Superior Publishing Company
A B C D E F G H

Library of Congress Card Catalog Number: 66-25423

PRINTED IN THE UNITED STATES OF AMERICA

*"Snatch from the ashes of your sires
    The embers of their former fires;
And he who in the strife expires
    Will add to theirs a name of fear
That tyranny all quake to hear. . . ."*
                                        — Byron

Foreword

Breathes there a man with soul so dead who never as a small boy said, "Golly, I'm going to be a fireman when I grow up." It was the American Dream before man started living on gasoline and sprouting wings. Not all those kids grew up to become firemen but, by golly, a lot of them never grew up, either.

I was one of those after-school pests the firemen in that F Street firehouse in Lincoln, Nebraska, must have wanted to see slide down the brass pole and land on his head. The only fire fighting I got to do was trying to pull a hot Roman candle out of my shirt one Fourth of July but, hanging around that station, I surely learned all about 4-alarms and black air and ladder hooks and sometimes my good friend Louie let me spread hay for the horses. Wistfully, I consider those yesterdays.

The romance of fire fighting still clings to the boy and man. Why else would there be gasolines called Fire Chief, fire trucks and fire hats popular for toys and play? Do you know there are fire buff societies in every large city in the nation with thousands of members? And in many museums you'll find replicas of the old fire station complete with drop harness and everything but the stable smell.

So I hope men who got to be firemen and a lot of the ones who didn't will buy this book or get it for birthdays or anniversaries of the founding of Mercury Hook and Ladder Co. No. 3. And I hope they'll have tender memories of those dear old days, of such goings on as the boys' rescuing that yellow cat from the back room of Duff's Saloon, clipping off the singed hair and keeping it for a mascot under the name of Arson.

In collecting material for this book I received splendid cooperation, as I always have, from libraries, historical societies and other picture sources. Of special help were Enid Thompson, librarian, and Kathleen Pierson, photo custodian, State Historical Society of Colorado; Opal Harber of Denver Western Library; Grace Dobbins, Salt Lake Public Library, and Margaret Shepherd, photo curator of Utah State Historical Society; Willard Ireland, archivist, and Barbara McClelland, librarian, Provincial Archives of British Columbia; Robert Monroe, head Special Collections, University of Washington Library.

I extend my public thanks to these people and to others equally helpful — John Barr Tompkins, head Public Services at Bancroft Library, University of California; Larry Booth, Title Insurance and Trust Co. Photo Lab in San Diego and Jerry MacMullen of that city; Betty Bender, librarian, Eastern Washington State Historical Society in Spokane; Burnby M. Bell, Clatsop County Historical Society, Astoria, Oregon; Marcia Tucker, Public Relations, Fireman's Fund Insurance Companies, San Francisco; Clara S. Beatty, director, Nevada Historical Society; Mary K. Dempsey, librarian, Montana Historical Society.

RALPH W. ANDREWS

BY RALPH W. ANDREWS

THIS WAS LOGGING
GLORY DAYS OF LOGGING
THIS WAS SEAFARING
(with Harry A. Kirwin)
THIS WAS SAWMILLING
REDWOOD CLASSIC
FISH AND SHIPS
(with A. K. Larssen)
HEROES OF THE WESTERN WOODS
INDIAN PRIMITIVE
CURTIS' WESTERN INDIANS
INDIANS AS THE WESTERNERS SAW THEM
PICTURE GALLERY PIONEERS
THE SEATTLE I SAW
PHOTOGRAPHERS OF THE FRONTIER WEST

CONTENTS

"FIRE! FIRE! FIRE!" 10

Red Shirts and Leather Helmets 11
VOLUNTEER FIREMEN . . . BUCKET BRIGADES . . .
HOSE REELS
Fires in Colorado — Nevada —
San Francisco — Utah

Fire Bell in the Night 73
FIRES IN MONTANA — ALASKA — BRITISH COLUMBIA

Pumpers and Pride 99
EARLY PUMPING ENGINES
Fires in Washington

Fighting Fires and Each Other 141
RACES AND CONTESTS ON AND OFF DUTY

"Here Come the Horses" 147
HORSE POWER . . . STEAMERS . . . HEAVY RIGS
Fires in Oregon

Bunk Rooms and Brass Poles 173
LIFE IN THE FIRE HOUSES

Trucks Get There Faster 185
TRUCKS ROLL PAST THE HORSES

Index 189

Photo Credits 192

"FIRE! FIRE! FIRE!"

"How often have you heard that cry, reader, and felt that there is no sound within the capability of human utterance so pregnant with startling emotion, and suppressed dismay, as fire. Wherever, or whenever the sound is heard, in country, town or city, on land or sea, by day or night, it is suggestive, spontaneously, of misery, terror, destruction and death. To the business man it falls upon the heart like a funeral knell, lest the fair hopes, long-cherished plans, and long-toiled-for prosperity are about to be swept from his sight, and the labor of years laid in ashes at his feet. He stops his breath while he counts the ominous strokes of the City fire bell; or the loud cries of the populace proclaim the locality of the fire; and either blesses God that he has once more escaped the ravages of the relentless enemy, as he offers up a silent hope or prayer that it may not be a particular friend who resides in the locality of the fire, and of whom he immediately thinks; or, he hurries on to the scene of action to remove the more valuable of his treasures, or those of his friend, and render aid at such a time, even to an enemy.

"Now all is excitement — the red glare around and upon the sky, and the black volumes of curling smoke rolling past, invite all haste; streams of men, engines, hose-carriages, hooks and ladders, are hurrying on, on, alike heedless of consequences to those who thoughtlessly impede their progress. The loud orders of the foreman through his trumpet; the solemn and alarming tolling of the bells; the impatience of the living tide of men eagerly pressing forward to the conflict, unite to give a fearful impetus to an almost superhuman effort. Soon — aye, how very soon! — but a few minutes apparently, and the gallant firemen — the guardians of the public property — with their means of salvation, and without a selfish thought, are at hand to compel submission to the common enemy.

"See them in their Roman-like helmets, and with their Roman — no, American — courage, hurrying up ladders; leaping on the roofs; rushing through doorways; climbing through windows; creeping on floors to prevent suffocation; crawling on the very top of the trembling and consuming building; that, in the front of the battle, they may successfully combat and annihilate the fell destroyer. What though he may fall over into immediate death; or drop through into the fiery abyss which is raging below, to immediate destruction; nothing daunted, on, on he presses; nor will he quit his post until the victory is won! . . ."

. . . from a feature article by D-R D-N in the August 1857 issue of "Hutching's California Magazine."

CITY FIREMEN Gleason, Brown, Downey in Spokane, Washington.

Red
Shirts
and
Leather Helmets

They had only one hose reel on a two-wheel jumper with six men on the drag rope. But they had helmets — black and red and the foreman was getting a white one expressed from St. Louis next week. All six men had pretty, red flannel shirts and there were a lot of canvas buckets around. But listen, old sport — you know what they had that was most important of all? They had guts and pride and a sense of importance. They were keeping other people alive and protecting property. They belonged.

Who were these six volunteer firemen in Canyon Springs? Well, Curley Butler was a blacksmith and Red Mattern was a bartender at the Acme. Alvin Schultz was a sort of lawyer, Flem Toogood ran a hoist up at the mine when he was sober and Pete Elwood was a faro dealer. Armand Settles was a banker and if you don't think all this made for democracy you never lived in a western mining camp in the '70s. Red could tell his wife to tell Al Shultz' wife she needn't put on airs because her husband was no better with a fire axe on a ladder than he was. That was one of the rewards of losing sleep, getting your beard singed and having to look at all those dead horses when the livery stable burned. There wasn't any pay in it but there were thrills and glory and prestige. This was public duty. They were firemen.

There may have been flaws in the old volunteer fireman system but nobody came up with a better one until more people invented more equipment, provided more water and more money to save more lives and buildings. Volunteer companies were strictly homespun but they did the job they had to do most of the time if it was at all possible. And if the preacher's wife started a movement "to keep those young boys away from those awful rowdy firemen who play cards and spit tobacco," the other faction could always say, "What if they do gamble for jackstraws and jingling money? They gamble with their lives every time you call for help, Mrs. Perkins." And if they could remem-

11

ber it, they might recite that poetry somebody wrote:

"The fireman from his slumbers waking,
  At once his quiet home forsaking,
Regardless of both health and life,
  Rushes to the deadly strife.
While still the cry of wild despair
  Is wafted on the midnight air,
    Fire! Fire! Fire!"

So as long as the hotel and livery barn were made of pine boards and you could start a fire by rubbing two prospectors together, you had to have hell-for-leather smoke chasers to break into a blazing room and rescue a baby or old crippled Dan or Susie Clements' rag doll. And they had to be the kind that could bat their eyes open in the middle of the night at the first clang of the fire alarm six blocks down Alder Gulch or leave the table with a mouthful of range beef and be going like sixty when they reached the front stoop. They might be refugees from hard work most of the time but when they were pulling down a wall with fire behind it, they could crawl out from under a pile of red-hot embers and grin. Call the volunteer firemen all the names you want to but don't forget to call them in plenty of time for the Fourth of July parade.

From the '50s to the '80s there were all kinds and sizes of western communities and all sorts and varieties of volunteer firemen, but there was only one enemy—the Fire Fiend, the Red Hand of Death, the Raging Inferno. Once the alarm sounded, the boys had to jump lively from whatever they were doing, run hell-bent to the fire station, grab helmets, tools and equipment and get to the fire on the double. On almost every run there was dubious encouragement from long-legged boys racing ahead of them, whooping and hollering, dogs barking alongside of them and getting under their feet but it all added up to a "Fireman, save my child" excitement that had a lot of pride buttoned up under those red shirts.

Those red shirts. They also added to the excitement yet they meant far more than that. They were splashes of color that symbolized the business the wearers were in, red of shirt and fire that had attraction for every wide-eyed youth and blue-eyed lass. The red shirt was a badge of office, visual proof to all and sundry that the man inside it belonged to that select and daring group—the fire fighters.

And to a lesser degree, the fire hat served to identify the man with derring-do, although it had a considerable utilitarian function. The thick, hard leather protected a man's head from falling bricks and debris, the long rear projection kept water from running down his neck, and when he turned it around, it shielded his face from extreme heat. And if he had no axe or club, he could smash a pane of glass with a hefty swipe of the heavy, almost unbreakable helmet. For parades and dress purposes, brass or nickel badges or shields, carrying some name or insignia of the company, were often mounted on the front.

It took some time for it to come about but the Ladies Temperance Society finally admitted the volunteer firemen did do some good.

"WE STRIVE TO SAVE," says banner carried by Nanaimo, British Columbia, volunteer fire crew, Sept. 28, 1894.

(Above) FIRE BRIGADE. Revelstoke, British Columbia.

(Right) VOLUNTEER Fire Department. Spokane, Washington, 1886.

(Above) HAVRE FIRE DEPARTMENT, 1910. (Below) Helena Fire Department about 1880—both in Montana. (Right) Circle City, Alaska, Fire Department.

(Above) GEORGE M. OTTING-
ER, Chief of Salt Lake City Volunteer Fire Department 1876-83
and first chief of paid department. (Below) One of Salt Lake's
first engines.

(Opposite, top) FIRE BRIGADE No. 2 at Meiggs Wharf, San Francisco, California, 1855, from ambrotype. (Left) Helena, Montana, fire department, 1876.

(Bottom row, left to right) TABOR HOSE CO. No. 5, Denver, Colorado; first paid department in Spokane, Washington, 1889; Nanaimo, British Columbia, volunteer fire department, 1894.

(Above) VIRGINIA CITY, Nevada, firemen on C
Street with new pumping engine in 1862. (Below)
Williams Creek fire brigade in Barkerville, British
Columbia, in 1870s.

18

(Right) CANON CITY, Colorado, volunteer fire company about 1879. (Below) Hart Hook and Ladder truck in San Diego, California, 1887.

(Above) HOSE REEL used by Helena, Montana, fire department in early years starting with 1876.

(Bottom row) HOSE REEL at left and Seattle fire-fighting crew after 1889 fire. (Center) Chief James Devine of Salt Lake City Fire Dept., 1894. (Right) Howard Engine Co. No. 3, San Francisco—organized June 15, 1850, disbanded Dec. 1, 1866.

(Above) SILVER PLUME, Colorado, hose cart No. 1 and 1884 pumper.

PALACE DRUG STORE and Midland Ticket Office reduced to hot ashes in Cripple Creek's April, 1896, fire.

COLORADO

The boilers burst and bleu

FEW STICKS OF FURNITURE are all that remains of the Cripple Creek meeting hall.

Cripple Creek wide open . . .

The town that "should have been shipping cattle" for thousands of dollars but found itself dealing in gold bullion running into the millions, had its baptism of fire in April 1896. And where it should have been satisfied with one fire that burned fifteen hundred people out of their homes and businesses, it had to have two within a week that pushed the total of the homeless to five thousand. This was Cripple Creek, the boom town that never did anything by halves.

April 25, 1896, started out as a pleasant Saturday in the Colorado high country but by midafternoon twenty acres of it were in ruins. In the six years of its phenomenal rise to riches and prominence the town had boosted gold production to $20 million and people were working hard as well as living high. The hotels, stores and saloons—all wooden buildings, most of them false-fronted and flimsy— were jampacked with spenders; the opera house, gambling rooms and dance halls getting ready for another big night.

Then, the story goes, a fire started in a room over the Central Dance Hall. A bartender and

a woman got into an argument which developed into slaps and punches and in the melee a kerosene stove was tipped over. The oil caught fire, spread quickly over the carpet and board floor and within seconds was out of control. Hot tempers were lost in hotter flames, the man and woman fleeing out on Myers Avenue to spread the news.

Cripple Creek had a volunteer fire department and by the time the butcher, clerk and blackjack player had dropped cleaver and cards to pick up fire axe and water bucket and run the hose reel to the Central Dance Hall, it was a towering mass of flames with occupants screaming at the upper floor windows. Girls of convenience threw out their belongings and slid down rope fire escapes or jumped into the throngs on the board sidewalks. Water pressure ran low, the roof fell in and sparks were caught by the wind to start more fires on adjoining streets.

Banks, saloons and hotels were consumed in the voracious march of the fire as the wind took it up the hill into the district of elegant homes and on across to the railroad depot. Fire equipment came rumbling by train from the neighboring camp of Victor but found itself powerless against the mad violence of the red demon. And once the wind sagged, the flames

(Opposite) EL PASO LIVERY BARN burning in Cripple Creek, Colo. April, 1896.

23

returned to where they started at Myers and Third to lick up the shacks and crib houses, more saloons and stores.

By early afternoon thirty acres of Cripple Creek were in smoking ruins, thousands of residents out of homes, jobs and money, considering the sorry remains with weary, smoke-smarting eyes. Emergency quarters were whacked together, the hungry and homeless fed and sheltered. In three days permanent rebuilding had started, the girls were back in their bed-and-washstand rooms and almost everybody felt glad the fire stopped when it had.

Only it hadn't. Flushed with success, it started up again in the "broomstraw" Portland Hotel when grease caught fire on a kitchen range. Dry wood and wind combined to show cocky Cripple Creek what a fire could really be like. The hotel roof crashed down, a geyser of sparks and glowing brands shot up and the town was sprayed in a hailstorm of fireworks. This explosion was quickly followed by two more—the bursting of the Palace Hotel's overheated boilers and the blast of half a ton of stored dynamite. Myers, Bennett and other streets were glutted with terror-stricken men, women and children, horse and mule teams. A stagecoach driver ten miles from Cripple Creek reported he and his passengers could see flames shooting a hundred feet in the air.

All afternoon the wind kept fanning the fury until restaurants, meat and general stores, land offices, saloons, stables and more saloons were licked out of existence. In panic, people clawed their way up the hill to the safety of the reservoir while down below them firemen battled to keep the hospital intact.

When the wind finally stopped blowing, the fire died down and people began taking a few deep breaths—but not the thousands who were burned out and worn out. Food stocks had been destroyed and those left were attacked by the hungry hordes which could not wait for relief trains already on the way.

When the trains arrived, the town committees were ready to distribute food supplies, cooking utensils and tents. Relief workers handed out medical goods and herded the women and children into churches and homes still standing. From Colorado City and Colorado Springs more trains were sent and as the homeless were cared for, hammers and saws were doled out to everybody who could nail up boards. Disasters could strike and fire could

(Above) THEY BLEW UP THE DENVER HOUSE to keep fire from spreading farther. Cripple Creek, April 1896.

(Opposite) BENUMBED CITIZENS view ashes of Cripple Creek stores.

burn but there was still gold underfoot where Bob Womack had found it, millions of dollars there for the digging. The spirit of the new day in Cripple Creek was—"Let's get on with it!"

LAUNDRY WAGON HORSE shies and citizens watch Cripple Creek fire raging a block away, April 1895.

(Above) CLEANING UP Cripple Creek after devastating fire of April, 1896.

(Below) CRIPPLE CREEK businesses crowd into one of few buildings left standing in this part of town.

(Above) CRIPPLE CREEKERS pause for pose after 1896 fire at Burnett and 4th Streets.

(Below) SMOKING RUINS of Tutt and Penrose Block. Close detail of standing building on page 30.

(Below) APRIL 1896 FIRE in Cripple Creek swept through this building — only one left standing on Bennett Street.

TUTT AND PENROSE BLOCK was left in shambles by Cripple Creek fire. Expanded view bottom page 28.

30

RUINS OF JIMTOWN (Old Creede), June 5, 1892.

And Jimtown lay in ashes

An explosion in a small wooden building set it on fire and in two hours the booming mine town of Jimtown was almost totally destroyed. Whipping up the gulch on the hot morning of June 5, 1892, the fire swept through building after building, leaving hundreds of miners homeless and accounting for seven deaths.

"The scene . . . was one of wildest excitement," reported the Denver *Republican* the next day. "Merchants who had residences on the hills tumbled out and tried to save what they could. . . . The heat became unbearable and little could be done by the salvage corps. Creede Avenue and Cliff Street were soon a mass of flames, and the smoke and heat made it impossible to save much.

"The lawless element made a raid on the saloons, robbing them of quantities of liquors. . . . By 8 o'clock the fire had spent its fury and was all out in two hours, wiping out the entire town of Jimtown.

"Between the Brainard and Beebe Hotel, on North Second Street, on the school section on the south, the bluffs on the east, and the second bench of the hill on the west, all is a total and complete ruin . . . beyond heaps of burned hardware, rolls of corrugated iron, and the ashes and debris of $1,000,000 worth of building and goods.

"It has been a wild and heart-sickening scene in the camp today. Hundreds of families are homeless, and with their few household goods are scattered about the barren patches of the school land on the mercy of their friends or charity until they can find shelter. . . .

"Following the fire a wild debauch was entered into by the sots and fast women of the camp. Free liquors were had for the stealing, and many cases of wines, bottles of whiskey, boxes of cigars, and such goods were seized and hundreds were drunk before the flames had half burned down. Mayor Morton found one drunken reveler in his livery barn attempting to set fire to the hay. He was invited by the incendiary to assist, but instead he knocked him down with his gun. . . ."

31

CALAMITY STRUCK SILVER PLUME, Colorado, at 1 a.m. one night in 1884, reducing it to ruins, killing one person and rendering hundreds homeless.

Silver Plume was mass of ruins

"The Smouldering Plume" headlined the story in a local newspaper of 1884. "Entire Business Portion of Town Burned . . . Scores Homeless and Penniless . . . Patrick Barrett Burned Alive."

"The thriving little town of Silver Plume," continued the story in extravagant phrase, "is to-day a mass of ruins and ashes. In a few brief hours there disappeared about fifty beautiful little residences and substantial business houses, in which were invested, in many cases, the earnings of a lifetime of toil, and men, women and children are cast upon the world to-day, destitute of all but the scant clothing worn upon their bodies, having neither home or money.

"About one o'clock this morning, while the citizens of our neighboring town were reposing, unconscious of the terrible calamity destined to visit them, they were awakened by excited cries of 'Fire.' It was discovered that flames were issuing from the rear of the saloon run by Sam Demott, on the corner of Main and Charles Streets. Efforts were made to quench the fire, but the elements had gained the mastery of the situation, and began to spread rapidly. Adjacent buildings were soon ignited, and the vast volumes of smoke, gigantic, crackling flames and shooting sparks convinced the citizens that a great conflagration was upon them. The members of the Silver Plume hook and ladder company were soon at work, but their efforts were fruitless: Everybody realized the town's helplessness in battling such a monster without water works, fire-engine or hose company.

"A messenger was finally despatched to Georgetown to secure aid, and the fire-bells immediately brought our firemen together. The Star Hook and Ladder Co's. truck, drawn by four horses, soon afterwards arrived upon the scene. In the meantime the destroyer was marching west on Main Street, devouring in its path the buildings on each side of the street, after having laid low the residences and business houses in the vicinity where the fire originated, including the Coloradoan office. The conflagration had reached almost to the creek, which it threatened to cross and strike terror to the habitants of the southern end of town. The flames were also consuming the hotel next to the Catholic Church. The Dobson House was a mass of flames, Egan's and Cornish's halls were beds of coals, and the scene was exciting and affecting. Men whose little fortunes had disappeared in the smokes of the morning were desperately running here and there, crowds were rescuing goods from burning stores, teams and wagons were conveying them to places of safety, citizens were heroically battling the fiery serpent which hissed defiance in its terrible work, women and children were clinging to each other in fright as they witnessed the destruction of all they owned, buildings were being torn down and blown up with powder in order to save others, while above all were to be seen the forms of Georgetown's fire-laddies—the noble rescuers, to whom the Silver Plume citizens are indebted for saving the western section of town. When the hand fire-engine from Georgetown, accompanied by a hose-cart, was driven into the unfortunate village, the citizens became hopeful. In a few minutes the course of the flames was checked, and further destruction prevented.

"When the light of morning fell upon the town, it presented a sad scene of desolation and revealed the fact that not only were the losses of the night in property, but human life. The charred remains of Patrick Barrett were found in the ashes of the building in which he was sleeping when flames grappled him in their deadly embrace.

"It is the general opinion that the fire was the result of incendiaryism. On last Tuesday night two attempts were made to fire the saloon of Jennings & Boise, but both proved futile. This did not become known until last night, when a report was circulated upon the streets that a third attempt had been made to burn the town. It was not surprising, therefore, to those who had heard these reports when the fire broke out this morning. The citizens are very much excited, and if the guilty one is found, he will certainly participate as principal actor in a special neck-tie sociable."

GOLD-COIN MINE
BURNING, VICTOR'S
BIG FIRE, AUG. 21~1899.
YELTON PHOTO NO 86

PHOTO BY G. L. J.

"THE HOMELESS"
VICTOR'S BIG FIRE
AUG 21~1899
YELTON PHOTO   NO. 861

(Opposite) GOLD COIN MINE BURNING. Two views of fire in Victor, Colo., Aug. 21, 1899.

(Above) HOMELESS OF VICTOR after big fire of Aug. 21, 1899.

Reign of terror in Central City

"A terrible fire is now raging in Central City," ran a wire dispatch printed in the Boulder, Colorado, *News* on May 22, 1874, "that cannot possibly be checked until most of the city is gone. Most of the business houses on the east side of Main Street are already consumed and all the frame buildings on the opposite side of the street are in flames.

"A reign of terror almost prevails among the citizens. Men are working to save goods as it would be impossible to save property. The fire is now working its way toward the Teller House."

A report from Black Hawk at 1:15 p.m. gave later details. "The fire is still raging furiously with slim chances of saving any of town. The wind is blowing down the gulch toward Black Hawk and as there is a mile of buildings in the gulch between the two cities it is doubtful if either can be saved unless assistance arrives on time.

"The buildings already burned are: all the buildings on the east side of Main Street from Crawford's Drug Store to the end of Spring Street, all the buildings on opposite side including Thatcher, Stanley and Co. bankers, Boswell and Co., John Best, Seller and Sauer, Fred Gessler, J. H. Heuse, J. H. Schweden, are burned out on Main Street. On Lawrence St. —the theater, Concert Hall, Wells Fargo Co., Snyder's Bakery, Charot's Restaurant a n d many others. A number of residences on High St. are in flames and the Catholic school house and a number of buildings adjoining, on the street back of Main, have been leveled to the ground. The Teller House was on fire when your reporter left Central. Assistance is expected from Golden in the shape of fire engines."

At 2:15 came another bulletin from Denver: "A special train with Babcock Hook and Ladder No. 1 and our gallant fire boys were enroute to Golden." The *News* added the line—"Latest information is that the Teller House was saved."

The May 27 issue of the *Weekly Rocky Mountain News* gave the loss of property as $500,000 and further details. "The fire originated about 10:30 a.m., perhaps a few minutes later, in a Chinese wash house, or laundry, on Spring street. The air at the time was perfectly still, scarcely a ripple to disturb its serenity. For this reason it was nearly twenty minutes before the fire broke through and communicated with adjoining sheds and outhouses. From the best information obtainable, it appears tolerably certain that the Asiatics were engaged with their women is some sort of heathen worship, or celebration of rites only known to themselves, in which an iron or tin vessel filled with burning coals or combustibles figured prominently. This being accidentally overturned, or some of its matter otherwise thrown upon the floor, set the room into a blaze.

"Both of the local fire companies set themselves to work energetically to i s o l a t e the dwelling from the sheds and tinder boxes around it, so as to prevent its spread to the more thickly settled parts of the city on Main, Lawrence and upper Spring Streets. They succeeded in leveling most of the fire, but as soon as the flames broke through the Chinese quartel, they leaped with frightful impetuosity from roof to roof, until it seemed as though the main portion of the town was but one vast ocean of fire. It rushed up Spring to Bridge Street, crossing the gulch meanwhile, and attacking the rears of the row of frame mercantile houses fronting on Main, swept them out of existence in a few moments, divided its strength here, one column moving rapidly t o w a r d Nevada Street, swallowing up everything within reach on Bridge, Spring, Nevada and Main.

"Attacking the O. K. store, the chariot of flames tore madly down the street, consuming with the velocity of a whirlpool all that had been left to consume, leaped wildly up the bluff to Pine, and soon had everything on the street in ashes but the granite church of the Catholics. Reaching Lawrence, the main column of destruction jumped across the Concert hall, the express office and theater, roaring, shrieking and crushing its way through these, then leaving the massive sheet to assail the Register building, the principal torrent passed down Lawrence, attacking both sides, scattering devastation to every combustible thing, but Freas' and Raynolds' fire-proof, within its path, until checked at the burnt district of 1874 where there was nothing for it to feed upon."

(Above) WELLS FARGO Express office stands in ghostly eminence as smoke still rises from Central City ruins, May 21, 1874.

(Below) Mining town as it looked prior to million-dollar holocaust.

Searchlights from the militia camp shot through the night gloom as rifle and machine gun fire raked the miners' tents. Trying to escape the hail of bullets, some women and children fled to the cover of boxcars on the railroad siding, the men following them with guns to draw fire from the soldiers. Others huddled in the holes in the tent floors as militiamen set the canvas on fire and flames leaped high above the screams.

This was Ludlow, Colorado, on the night of April 20, 1914 when 20 men, women and children died in one of the "black days" of mining history. Today a monument rises from one of the shelter holes that dotted the tent city. The inscription reads:

> "In memory of men, women and children who lost their lives in freedom's cause at Ludlow, Colorado, April 20, 1914. Erected by the United Mine Workers of America."

This account written from story by William Logan in Denver "Rocky Mountain News" of April 19, 1964.

And the prairie wind blows through the pinion and sagebrush.

The strike by 12,200 miners started on Sept. 23, 1913. Miners and their families were forced to leave company-owned housing at the mines in the canyons to the west. They walked in long lines down the dusty roads to the six tent colonies set up for them on the flat lands from Walsenburg to Trinidad by the United Mine Workers union, the largest at Ludlow. This was a settlement on the Colorado and Southern Railroad, 14 miles north of Trinidad, composed of a depot, saloon, post office and school for the children of the few residents.

To maintain the peace, the Colorado National Guard was sent into the area. This was composed of family men who could not leave their work indefinitely and as they went home, they were replaced by professional strikebreakers imported by the mining interests.

During the six months that followed, strikers and families tried to live as normally as the

40

loody Ludlow massacre

EMBATTLED MINERS stand massed for military resistance to expected attack by Colorado National Guard, April 1914.

menace of the nearby soldiers' encampment allowed. In the 100 tents at Ludlow they ate, slept, washed clothes and vowed to resist at all costs the tyranny and threats imposed on them by the gun fighters in the guise of guardsmen. Warned by occasional rifle shots, wary miners dug holes under the tents as "escape routes" in case of bad trouble. It was all a brave show for bad trouble came and with it disaster in the ten-day civil war.

On April 19 the Ludlow men were playing a baseball game and saw six men with rifles riding up. They sat on their horses calling threats until one rode closer. "Have your fun today," he shouted. "We'll have ours tomorrow." If it was fun, they had it.

The trouble was presaged by a telephone call from a commander of a National Guard detachment to the leader of the strikers, Louis Tikas. The officer demanded the surrender of a boy who, he claimed, was being held against his will in the strikers' camp.

Tikas sensed danger and telephoned the chief union official in Trinidad that there might be trouble. He went to the National Guard commander at the depot and again denied there was anyone in the camp who was there against his will. While he was walking the several hundred yards back to the tent colony, three blasts of dynamite exploded in the militia camp, interpreted as a signal to launch an attack.

It came at once, militia machine guns raking the miners' tents. Some of them grabbed guns and ran out of the colony to positions along the railroad embankment, returning militia fire. While Leader Tikas telephoned the union leader to warn other strikers' groups, the armed miners kept on shooting, hoping to draw the guardsmen's fire away from the tent colony.

Late in the afternoon their ammunition began running low and they looked for help from Trinidad where 500 miners were reported to be organizing an armed relief crew. With

(Left) THREAT LETTER sent to informer by strikers. (Right) LUDLOW TENT COLONY near Trinidad, Colorado, occupied by striking United Mine Workers of America and families.

only a few rounds of cartridges left, strikers prepared to evacuate the tents and ran for the cover of railroad cars as women and children made for an arroyo.

One unarmed miner, William Snyder, told of being under fire in Ludlow and of the death of his small son. His statement was found in the National Archives among records of the Federal Commission on Industrial Relations, some 40 years after the massacre.

"I heard about three signal blasts from the soldiers' camp," he wrote. "Then about 20 or 30 cavalrymen crossed the tracks and took up positions with their guns. Our men went to the side of the tracks to keep them away from women and children. The other side fired first. Then the battle was on.

"I was unarmed and I stayed in our tent with my family. We were in our cellar, just a hole in the ground. About 4:30, when the shooting died down for a while, my boy got out of the hole to get his little sister some water. She was begging for it. It seemed safe enough.

"He was sitting in a chair in our tent which was like lace from all the shooting, and was reaching over to kiss his little sister who was between his knees when a bullet struck him above the temple on the right side and blew his brains out."

Militia men rushed the tents some time after 6 p.m. and set the tents on fire. Leader Tikas was arrested, beaten on the head with a rifle and then shot by guardsmen who said he was trying to escape. The entire tent colony was burned to the ground, nothing remaining but a smouldering ruin studded with stoves, blackened bed springs, charred bodies, dogs, chickens and pitiful remnants of the families' belongings.

Machine gun and rifle fire was kept up all during the next day and no medical workers or undertakers were allowed into the area. When they were permitted to carry off the dead, they found the bodies of 11 children and two women in one of the dugouts. These and those to follow were the "black days" of Colorado mining that neither miners nor owners ever forgot.

42

CAMP BESHOAR, military headquarters of UMA workers.

(Above) STRIKERS' FAMILIES in Forbes Tent Colony. (Opposite, top) Some members of same group after colony was ravaged by militia and fire, April 1914. (Below) Another view of Forbes Tent Colony after devastation.

Hole Where Bodies
Of 11 Children And
2 Women Were
Recovered From
After Fire At Ludlow
Tent Colony
Dold

After The Battle At Southwest

Red Cross Members Searching Ruins Ludlow Tent Colony

Near View Of Ruins
Ludlow Tent Colony
Dold

(Opposite, top left) BLACK HOLE OF LUDLOW where two women, eleven children died in fire. (Center and above) After battle at Southwestern Mine. (Opposite, bottom) Red Cross workers searching ruins at Ludlow Tent Colony. (Center and below) Ruins at Ludlow, April 19, 1914.

Chavez's Hole After Fire
Ludlow Tent Colony
Dold

NEVADA

"A fearful gale was blowing

"The greatest fire in Eureka occurred on April 19, 1879. At about one o'clock in the morning of that date, while a fearful gale was blowing, a fire broke out in the green-room of Bigelow's Opera House, from the explosion of a lamp. The flames spread to the *Sentinel* building, the Masonic Hall and the Western Union Telegraph Office, and by the winds were blown east and north, down Buel, Spring and Main Streets. The Jackson House and the front portion of V. B. Perry's saloon escaped by a miracle, but the remaining portion of the town embraced within the streets above named, was, within the period of two hours, a mass of blackened ruins, and the fire was only checked when it reached the end of Main Street at the foundry, Spring Street above Mrs. Dennis', and Paul Street at its terminus. In all this area the only

property that escaped, excepting the two structures already mentioned, consisted of the fire-proof building of the *Sentinel* office and the vaults of Paxton's bank. Mr. Moch, proprietor of a restaurant, was fatally burned, and Frank Alderson received serious injuries. The Fire Department had battled manfully, but in vain. The total loss was estimated at $1,000,000; half the town lay in ashes, and two thousand people were destitute and homeless. Immediately after the conflagration, a remarkable journalistic feat was performed by the *Sentinel* force. The stone fire-proof building at the rear of the main office was so hot that the printers could remain in it only by shrouding themselves in wet blankets. Nevertheless they set up the paper and got out an edition before ten o'clock in the morning. To relieve the suffering of Eureka,

Accounts of Nevada fires are taken from "History of Nevada," edited by Myron Angel: Thompson and West, 1881.

HOLOCAUST IN GOLDFIELD, Nevada, one of many in early days. This fire in 1923 destroyed 40 blocks of homes and business buildings in famous mining camp.

that morning in Eureka . . . "

Governor Kinkead immediately placed at the disposal of the authorities of that town the sum of $1,500, which remained unexpended from a Legislative appropriation in aid of the Silver City sufferers. Public meetings were also held at Reno, Carson, and other points, and energetic steps were taken to collect and forward money and supplies. The smoke of the conflagration had scarcely passed away before the rebuilding of Eureka had been resolved upon, and in a few months the task had been completed with remarkable energy."

At about ten o'clock on the seventeenth of August 1880, another great fire began, breaking out at the rear of Mrs. Poplin's fruit and vegetable store on Main Street, and taking almost the same course as the conflagration of the previous year. Three hundred houses, many of them business establishments and some of them the finest private residences in town, were consumed. A space equal to fifty acres was swept almost completely. Only half a dozen buildings remained to relieve the scene of desolation . . . Jack Perry's corner, the Douglas Building, the Foley- Rickard Block, Paxton and Co's. bank, Jacob Cohn's store, Schneider's Drug Store and C. Lautenschlager's saloon. The *Leader* office, Odd Fellows Hall, theater, International Hotel, Vanina and Co's billiard saloon, A. M. Hillhouse's elegant residence and Methodist Episcopal Church were among the prominent buildings destroyed. But for the most determined effort of the firemen, the fire would not have been confined to the east of Main Street. No statement of the exact amount of the damage was ever published.

SKELETON WALLS remain after early morning fire in Reno's historic Riverside Hotel, March 15, 1922. The last to leave burning building was hotel cat which perched atop barroom door until forced out by smoke.

"*The flames seemed to leap across whole blocks...*" VIRGINIA CITY

"The combustible nature of the materials of which the towns are built, the terrific winds which daily visit this side of the mountains, with the dry character of the atmosphere, and the careless habits of the transient population, all combined to make the chances of a conflagration numerous. This was early seen by the resident population, and efficient means were taken, as it was thought, to prevent any widespread disaster. So thought the cities of Chicago and Portland, but the fire-fiend devoured them.

"The first great fire in Virginia City broke out August 29, 1863, in a carpenter shop in the rear of Patrick Lynch's saloon. About $700,000 worth of property was destroyed. The burned district extended from Taylor Street to Sutton Avenue, north and south, and from A Street to B, and partly down to C, east and west. This was then the principal business part of the town. This fire was the occasion for the culmination of the feud between the engine companies Number One a n d Two, m o r e particularly described in the account of the Fire Departments.

On September 29, 1865, a fire started at the Fountain Head Restaurant. It burned over an area extending from Union Street to below Sutton Avenue, and as far as D Street east, and A Street west. About $400,000 worth of property was destroyed.

On September 23, 1866, Music Hall was destroyed by a fire occasioned by the bursting of a lamp.

On the n i n e t e e t h of September, 1870, another fire broke out in Lonkey & Smith's lumber yard, corner of D and Smith Streets. It spread from D down to E Street east, and as far as A Street west, running close to Taylor Street on the north, and to the Tahoe House on the south. The total damage amounted to $300,000.

"June 29, 1873, at 11 o'clock, p.m., the Mc-Laughlin & Root building, on B Street, blew up and took fire; 100 pounds of Hercules powder, six cases of nitro-glycerine, 100 pounds of giant powder, and 200 pounds of common powder had b e e n stored under the bedroom of Major General Van Bokkelen, by that gentleman, and exploded. He was killed, also J. P.

Smith, W. D. Davis, Ben Mandel, Mrs. Ed. Dean and her little daughter, Billy Low, Chas. Knox, Mrs. Emily Connor and John Devine. Losses by fire, water, etc., $225,000. Many persons were wounded. A portion of the building was occupied by the Bank of California.

"The great fire, one long to be remembered, commenced at 5:30, a.m., October 26, 1875, in a low lodging-house on A Street, and resulted in the total destruction of the business part of the city, and a loss of about $12,000,000. The burned district included all between Taylor Street on the south, and Carson Street on the north, Stewart Street on the west, and the Chinese quarter on the east. The fire soon passed beyond all possibility of control, driving the firemen and people from one block to another with scarcely any delay. As the air became heated the flames seemed to leap across whole blocks at a time. The 'fireproof' buildings seemed to offer as little resistance as those of wood. The mills and hoisting-works were swept away as by a whirlwind. Considerable quantities of powder were stored around the town, and this exploding increased the horrors of the scene, and paralyzed the efforts to quell the fire or to remove valuables, so dangerous was it to approach a building.

"The shafts of the mines burned down to a considerable distance, occasioning much caving in. At the Ophir a cage was let down and covered with dirt to prevent the fire from passing down, but the fastenings or springs gave way when the dirt was shoveled on it, and the fire went down the shaft. The Consolidated Virginia saved their shaft with a bulk-head covered with dirt. Soon after the fire a gale commenced blowing, tumbling down the tottering walls and filling the air with clouds of ashes and cinders. November 2nd a snow storm set in and made the situation still worse.

"The people set to work to rebuild even while the beds of coals were glowing with heat, and in a few days most of the people were under shelter. The railroad brought in supplies of timber and provisions. Forty-s i x trains passed over the road in one day; 100 cars were dropped at Reno for Virginia City in one day."

"*Almost a hurricane was blowing that Sabbath morning . . .*" RENO

"The first serious fire occurred Wednesday, October 29, 1873, and ere it ceased its ravages destroyed more than 100 buildings. About half-past ten at night, flames were discovered issuing from the Western Hotel, on Commercial Row, between Virginia and Sierra Streets. The alarm was instantly sounded and people rushed from all directions to the scene of danger. Before the cisterns could be uncovered and the buckets brought, the flames had made great headway and were burning fiercely. The citizens fought desperately, but wet blankets and buckets of water seemed of little avail, and flames spread rapidly. The fire quickly reached Masonic Hall on the west and Barnett's brick block on the east. Around this it went to Virginia Street and down to Bell & Burke's brick store on Second Street. Crossing Virginia Street here it swept back on the other side to Commercial Row. In two hours were burned the two brick blocks bounded by Sierra, Center, Second and Commercial Row, except four stores, a few dwellings, the *Journal* office and the Masonic Hall, the very business heart of the city.

"Good service was rendered by the railroad fire trains that came rushing to the scene from Wadsworth and Truckee. The Carson City fire engine, S. T. Swift, also came, but owing to a delay of the train did not arrive until the fire was under control. The loss was estimated at $100,000, on which there was considerable insurance.

"In the evening of October 25, 1875, George Schaffer's residence on Commercial Row caught fire, and before the flames could be extinguished five dwellings were destroyed, with a total loss of $25,000.

"A few minutes after one o'clock on the morning of Februray 13, 1877, flames were seen issuing from the upper story of the Depot Hotel. The alarm was sounded and the Fire Department and engine No. 48 quickly appeared on the scene. The flames were extinguished after damaging the building to the amount of $15,000. Mrs. Lena Johnson, a Swede chambermaid, was unable to effect her escape and was burned to death. While the fire was burning fiercely the overland train from the East arrived, and passing the burning building safely, stopped just beyond to discharge its load and then went on.

"The great disaster that has befallen the courageous young city and the greatest event in her history, is the memorable fire of Sunday, March 2, 1879. Almost a hurricane was blowing that Sabbath morning, filling the streets with clouds of dust, when fire caught in a pile of cedar wood back of the Railroad House, supposed to have been caused by sparks blown from a chimney that had been burning out. The flames were observed by an old lady known as Grandmother Hogan, who emptied two tubs of water upon them, but the wind blew so fiercely that they soon got beyond her control.

"The Fire Department was called out and the steamer, hand engine and No. 48 all responded with alacrity. The efforts of the firemen and citizens were futile in the face of the wind, and for four long hours they fought the roaring and rapidly spreading flames without avail. The fire marched on until there was nothing more within its grasp to feed upon, and then died out. The burned district embraced ten blocks, including every business house in town, save two grocery stores. The Masonic Hall and Catholic School were both saved almost miraculously, although the Catholic Church was destroyed. Mrs. John Beck was burned in her house while endeavoring to save some of her property. Three tramps, named Charles Falner, James Fitzpatrick and Robert Irvine, met the same fate in E. C. McKinney's barn, and an Indian was burned in the Nevada State Flouring Mills.

"Hundreds were thus rendered homeless, and the supply of food for the city had been almost totally consumed by the hungry flames. That night large quantities of bedding and food were received from Carson, Virginia and other places, and the homeless made as comfortable as possible in the churches and dwellings that had escaped the flames. A relief committee was organized, and everything possible done to relieve the suffering. The next day a bill was introduced into the Legislature, at Carson, appropriating $10,000 for the relief of the sufferers, and received the Governor's signature within an hour. . . .

"The amount of insurance on this was but $194,600, leaving a total loss of over $700,000.

"Great as was this disaster, the energy and enterprise of the citizens was greater, and soon new stores and dwellings began to appear over the ashes of those that had passed away. So great was the change wrought in a few months that nearly all traces of the fire vanished from sight, and Reno appeared to be as busy and prosperous as before. But though the visible effects of the fire could be so quickly removed, the invisible ones could not, and Reno to-day is suffering in her business and commercial enterprises from severe losses of the great conflagration."

"*A terrible calamity befell the town . . .*" PIOCHE

"On the night of September 15, 1871, a terrible calamity befell the town. It was the anniversary of Mexican Independence and the citizens of that nation were glorifying the occasion with ball, bonfire, wine and song, when just after midnight flames were seen to issue from the rear of a restaurant on the upper part of Main Street, and though the air was unruffled by a breeze they had got under irresistible headway before the majority of the inhabitants were massed to oppose them. In vain were all attempts to arrest the progress of the fire. Nearly all of the houses being of a dry and resinous material, the furious flames swept them away in quick succession, until only heaps of ashes and smouldering embers marked the site of what two hours earlier was the most flourishing and progressive of mining towns.

"From 1,500 to 2,000 men, women and children were without roofs to shelter them, and many were in destitute circumstances. Still these were not the most melancholy incidents of the fearful catastrophe. 300 kegs of powder which were stored in the cellar of a leading mercantile house on Main Street exploded with a force that shook the mountains to their center, and with it went up one wild wail from all who witnessed the grand yet terrible spectacle. Rocks, timbers and every conceivable missile of death swept across Main and Meadow Valley Streets, and the crowd on the latter street was raked as if by grape and canister. Thirteen men were killed and forty-seven others seriously wounded. The loss in property was over half a million, but a trifle of which was insured.

"Undismayed and but momentarily discouraged by this annihilating blow, the sufferers set about rebuilding, and six months later the temporary structures had all disappeared, and Pioche City was again in existence, her limits extended, population increased, and having improvements of a more substantial character.

"On the afternoon of Sunday, May 5, 1872, the town was again visited by a destructive fire,

resulting in the loss of twelve buildings, and property estimated to be worth $50,000. No lives were lost.

"On the twenty-second of August, 1873, a flood occurred which caused damage to the citizens to the amount of $10,000. It was the effect of a terrible rainstorm, which for a time so blackened the sky that it was necessary to light lamps in the houses.

"Another rainstorm of less violence occurred in the summer of 1874. Again, in 1876, another destructive fire visited the town. Of it the Pioche *Record* said:—

"On the morning of May 3, 1876, Pioche was again visited by a destructive fire, burning nearly a block of buildings, partially, on the east side of Lacour and the west side of Main Streets. The fire commenced about three o'clock in the old unoccupied hurdy, or dance house, on Lacour Street, adjoining the *Journal* office, and was discovered by two men in the office who had just completed striking off the paper, and were about to retire. A general alarm was sounded, and the three fire companies were on hand as soon as possible. We noticed one of the boys having on a ruffled nightgown, showing that he did not waste any time going home to put on a red shirt. After an hour of hard struggle they got the best of the flames and extinguished them. Twenty-one buildings were burned, and the loss estimated at $40,000.'"

RAWHIDERS took to Hooligan Hill when brawling, year-old boom town burned on Sept. 4, 1908.

(Left) EARLY FIRE CHIEF of Helena, Montana, volunteer fire department, 1875.

(Below) P R O U D FIREMEN, smart horses and equipment in Goldfield, Nevada, in front of Esmeralda Co. courthouse and Fire Station No. 1. Men and apparatus would have been more effective in destructive fires of 1905 h a d there been enough water.

ASTORIA, OREGON, Volunteer Fire Department in 1895.

55

"The right arm of San Francisco"

In the extravagant phrase of the day, Frank Soule set the case for the volunteer firemen. In his *Annals of San Francisco* he wrote of the fires of 1849 to 1851 and the "dread alarums at whose sound men's hearts sank and a whole people mourned . . . the torch has been repeatedly lighted and there have been the same high winds to fan the flames to greater fury; but, except in isolated cases, the damage done has been but trifling. More—aye, everything is due in this connection to the unrivalled Fire Department.

"The enemy they have to encounter might fright a dozen armies. They are forlorn hopes, that have to storm the very batteries of the fire-fiend. Their hard-fought battles, their many victories, and the able defence and guard they exercise over their precious charge, have gained them, better than laurel or gold, the sincerest thanks and warmest attachment of their fellow-citizens. San Franciscans would laugh were it said that we flattered the fire department. Does a man praise his right arm for performing its wonderful functions? Yet the fire department is the right arm of San Francisco. At the ring of the alarm-bell, it is not alone the errand-boy, the counter clerk, or the rowdy corner loafer that start for a scene of temporary excitement. But the merchant-millionnaire springs from his cushioned seat; the judge leaves court and cases; the industrious mechanic drops his tools; editors, lawyers and doctors abandon quills, briefs and pills, and with pallid cheek but nervous sinews hurry their engines to the threatened spot. They are playing for a fearful stake. Men must be daring gamblers to foil the enemy they deal with. Honor to whom honor is due. Give it freely to the fire department and when to it, to the whole body of enlightened, public-spirited and prominent citizens. These are men prouder of their leathern capes than though they were bedecked with the toddery uniform of a militia general—men who have poured out their means with no stinting hand in the formation of the department. The volunteer system need not be abandoned for a *paid* fire organization. Nothing could replace the loss of an institution so highly valued. San Franciscans might get along w i t h o u t government—dispense with churches—abolish drinking houses and places of amusement—cease soldiering—g i v e over reading newspapers—or see without regret their gambling saloons vanish in the clouds. Pleasures are easily done without; but home—bread—years of toil—life itself, are not coolly and calmly to be tossed into the flames. . . ."

LAFAYETTE HOOK AND LADDER CO. NO. 2, San Francisco, organized in 1853 by French residents of city.

SAN FRANCISCO— *"The Great Fires of 1849-50-51"*

"The first 'great' fire occurred on the 24th of December, 1849. Some such calamity had been dreaded through the months of high winds, by all who took into consideration the exceedingly inflammable nature of the buildings. Thin boards, cloth, and paint were tempting inviters of the destroyer. When it did come, it spread like a pestilence; and although the windy season had passed, it consumed completely the most flourishing portion of the city. Dennison's Exchange, in which the fire originated was ceiled with cotton cloth, and that was painted. Instantly this was on fire, and the whole building was burning before the neighborhood was aroused, it being not quite yet six o'clock in the morning. Scarcely a breath of wind was stirring to fan the fiery flame. At once the citizens crowded to the scene. Then the din of a thousand voices arose amid the crash of falling frames, the jingling of battered windows, the sharp sound of axes; and above all this, the roar of the devouring element, which now surged wildly round the Parker House, from the windows and doors of which, at both ends, clouds of smoke rolled forth. Just then the cry of "stored powder" was raised, and a general *stampede* of five or six thousand persons ensued. So rapidly spread the flames, that the conflagration was at once like a lion broke loose, defying all control. On, and still onward, it went and spread — water, labor, powder, everything seemed powerless to stay it. Glutted at last, when half the square was in ashes, nothing but smoke from burning cinders, like the breath from the red nostrils of a dying monster, was to be seen, where so recently had stood the works of human skill and labor. More than a million dollars had been destroyed in the property thus turned to ashes.

"But those who had suffered did not wait for the embers to grow dim, and the cinders to disappear, before applying anew their native energy. At once new buildings were in process of erection — built — occupied, and the business of the section again travelling its former course almost before the smoke had sped away from sight. Four months rolled away, the city had revived, and prosperity smiled in all her streets. Even the blackened district, blasted by the fire of December, had put on a glow of health. Just then, on the morning of the 4th of May, 1850, the second great fire commenced, almost on the very site of the previous one, and within a few hours swept away three entire blocks, destroying property to the estimated amount of four millions of dollars. But, again, with more than former energy, the people went ahead, and within ten days from the time of the fire, more than half the burnt district was covered with new buildings. . . . The 14th of June, 1850, came, and with it the third of those dreadful devastations which seemed sent, like the serpent of old, to destroy the young Hercules in its cradle. This fire has been so fully spoken of elsewhere in this book, that it may be only necessary here to say, that it exceeded in extent and loss both of those which had preceded it. Like those, it was frightful, as well from its rapidity as from the completeness of the destruction. It was in a different location from the fires already noticed, being more to the south, and reaching to the bay. . . .

"At about four o'clock on the morning of the 17th of September, 1850, the startling cry of *'Fire! Fire!'* alarmed the wakeful, a n d aroused the sleeping, with a suddenness and terror that an earthquake could not have produced. Perhaps in no other place in the wide world could that fearful cry create at once such general alarm and terror, and throw every individual of the community into such sudden and overwhelming excitement. So many whirlwinds of destruction had swept over the devoted city at short intervals, and with such fearful strides, that the whole community was as excitable as if they had stood on the brink of a crater. In a few minutes the streets were full of people, and the fire companies were on a full run for the scene. But so rapidly did the flames spread, that for a long time all efforts to arrest them seemed utterly vain. . . .

"Below Kearny Street, the whole row on the east side was destroyed, with the exception of the Verandah. About one hundred and twenty-five buildings were consumed. The entire loss could not be ascertained with any

This account taken from "Annals of San Francisco"
by Frank Soule.

57

degree of accuracy. It was far less in proportion to the space burned over than at any of the previous fires, from the fact that a large portion of the buildings destroyed were of one story, and small. The total loss was estimated at amounts varying from two hundred and fifty thousand to one million of dollars. . . .

"To those who had leisure, and a position suitable to take a view of the whole sea of flame, and who could divest themselves of the sensations of pain incident to the occasion, it was a grand, a sublime sight. The entire city was illuminated with a fierce glow of light, and the surrounding hills sent back again its reflective brilliancy, accompanied by ten thousand echoes of crackling timbers, rushing flames, the quick strokes of the engines, rattling of carts and wagons, the wrenching of falling houses, the roar and tumult of thousands upon thousands struggling almost hopelessly against their dread enemy, which swayed to and fro in terrible mockery of human effort. The greedy flames shot forth their dry, forked, snake-like tongues, lapping at everything within their reach, as if conscious of their own malignity and power; licking at the windows and walls and house-tops; darting out horizontally through jaws of black smoke and teeth of sparkling cinders; rushing across alleys and streets and vacant lots; twisting or writhing in agony or delight, . . .

"Soon came the broad light of day, giving a still more strange and gorgeous mantle to the hillsides, crowded with busy, or gazing, or shocked human beings, and mingling its heavenly rays with those that held their revel dance amid the halls and household gods, and wrapped themselves about the works of labor and genius, like so many scarlet mantles. Through a sea of blood the sun seemed to rise and gaze upon the work, his great Titan eye glowering down upon the devoted city as if red with anger and offended majesty. Yet few saw it. The little things about, and near and dear to the brave struggling hearts, were of much greater importance than the great ones far away.

"When at length dwellings and chattels were in the dust, and smoking embers, and ashes, and occasional jets of not yet glutted flame alone indicated the sites of recent homes and busy marts, it was painful to see the ejected sufferers, men, women, and children, sad and tearful, clinging to the relics of late fortunes and firesides. The public square was literally crowded with whatever could be snatched from the hungry fire. Up to a late hour at night many persons were still there with the few remnants left from their former property and comforts. . . .

"So the rejuvenated giant grew and progressed. Above the ashes new dwellings arose. Where the flames had scarce ceased crackling, the hammer and the saw were heard, answering back to the stone-cutter's chisel and the earnest ring of the mason's trowel. Like the structures of the coral insect, the islands which rise from the ocean's depths, San Francisco grew upwards from her own ashes, supplanting the frosts of destruction with a crop of success. . . .

"But amid all this there lingered in the minds and memories of the people a feverishness and sensitive chord of apprehension that thrilled at the slightest alarm, like a spider's web when struck by an insect. The sound of the first stroke of a fire-bell was enough to clear church or theatre, or drowsy bed, in an instant. The dreadful scenes witnessed had inscribed their history deep and dark, and could not be erased. This proclivity to alarm had soon an ample cause of new exercise. The anniversary of the fire of May 4th, 1850, approached. Threats had been made, it was said, that it was to be signalized by a similar spectacle. . . .

"The sun had gone down over the western hills, and the dying sea-breeze wasted its last breath against the brow of night. The curtain had fallen upon the last scene of the last play, the lecturer had retired from the stand, the clergyman from the pulpit. The lawyer was dozing over his brief, and weary limbs had laid down on the sleeper's couch. The editor had put the last period to his leader, and turned from his flagging duties to tremble at the shrill outcry of *'Fire!'* That dreadful word in a moment found an echo on a hundred tongues, and the pealing bells and rushing engines answered back to the sound. It was nearly midnight on the eve of May 4th, 1851. The flame when first seen was in a paint-shop, on the south side of the plaza, and was not larger than a man's hand; but in five minutes, the whole upper story was one entire blaze.

"At first, the wind was but a breath; but it had scarcely lapped the flames, ere, like a tiger, after his first taste of blood, its whole nature awoke to the fiery carnival, and became an avenging and malicious spirit. It caught the black clouds of smoke and the flashing

(Right) **H. S. CROCKER BUILDING** on Bush Street, San Francisco, California.

(Below) **BALDWIN HOTEL FIRE**, San Francisco, California.

streaks of flame, and with a living skill twisted them into wreaths and festoons fit to adorn the brow of crumbling Sodom. As if its prison-bars had snapped with the first flame, and the doors of its cells had burst open, from every point of the compass its dread ministers poured forth, and joined the banquet in one general whirlwind, turning hotel and store, office and dwelling, into a fiery and dizzying waltz of conflagration. Nothing could stay the fury and progress of the united wind and flame. On, and still onward, through the hours of that dreadful night, it marched and rushed, and devoured, greedy and remorseless, while food could be found for the gnawing hunger of the destroyer. . . .

"The tornado of fire in its devouring path over the city furnished a scene of more grandeur, terror and sublimity, and, devoid of one's sympathies, of more beauty, than any other event which had transpired in our nation during the present century. And yet all of one's sensibilities were inevitably interested, and were necessary in order that this awful exhibition of nature in her wildest and most pitiless mood, should duly and perhaps profitably affect man through his more kindly qualities. The commencement of the fire was like the flash of gunpowder, so almost instantaneous was its spread. For a few moments, hope, fear and dread balanced upon the brakes of the engines. As those gallant philanthropists, the firemen, bent every thought, and strained each muscle, in a death contest with the common enemy, hope for an instant spoke of triumph. But physical exertions and prayers were unavailing — the city's doom had come. . . .

"The sight was sad, afflictive, awful. Great masses of smoke ascended and rolled away, loaded with the wealth of men, the rewards of toil and danger, bearing far above the crumbling city great flocks and sheets of burning cinders, and forming huge clouds touched with every tint, from clear white light to the darkness of night. Frame houses faded away like frost work. Brick structures became batteries of flame, and poured forth immense jets from their windows and doors. Iron and zinc curled up like scorched leaves, and sent forth their brilliant flames of green, blue and yellow tints, mingling with, and modifying the glare of the great red tongues of fire which flashed upwards from a thousand burning houses. The hillsides were lighted as if the sun were above the eastern mountains, and their trees, shrubs,

herbage, houses and people were as distinguishable in the bright light, as if it were noon. But darkness hung over a large portion of the shipping, where the broad and heavy ocean of smoke lay down in impenetrable gloom over the bay.

"People became paralyzed. Many removed their stocks of goods four or five times, and had them overtaken and destroyed by the flames at last. The streets were crammed with masses of human beings and rushing teams, only giving way before the advance of the elements, as the smoke, and heat, and crashing walls pushed them back. Men became mad. Some rushed headlong into the flames. Weeping women and prattling infancy were wandering amid ashes and destruction. Every few moments the earth and air trembled, as great buildings were torn into fragments by explosions of gunpowder, and the atmosphere was filled with shattered timbers, bricks and mortar. The multitude hung upon the borders of this 'vast sea of flame,' few, comparatively, knowing what were the dangers and exertions of those who were within the range of the stifling smoke and scorching heat. In less than nine hours from the beginning, more than twenty squares existed only in memory, and in the ascending columns of smoke and flame which covered the site of the city.

"The Union Hotel burned like a furnace until the woodwork was nearly destroyed, when the huge walls, five stories high, pitched headlong into the street, and over the wrecks of neighboring dwellings, long before they reached the earth, completely lost in the flames and smoke which ascended from below. So intense was the heat that jets of water poured from the hose became instantly converted into steam, or were licked up by the thirsty flames. . . .

"As a complete calamity there was scarcely a parallel. There had probably never been another so entire a destruction of a city since the burning of Moscow. More than three quarters of it had been blotted out. The destruction of property, the loss of life, the suffering, the privation, the ruin — complete a picture of so much misery as makes the heart ache to think of it. The loss could scarcely be exaggerated. One had to speak of millions. It was the greatest by far of any which had visited the city, and it was more disheartening because of its following so closely upon the track of the others. Almost the entire city had been the product of Californian industry. Very little foreign capital had been employed in erecting the buildings and improving the streets. It was the result of labor performed in one shape or another within the country itself. And it was a painful and disheartening circumstance to have all this blotted out in a single night.

"Her citizens met the disaster like men. The first shock naturally seemed to paralyze and drive them almost to despair. But when they reflected upon the causes which had made them, and remembered that they still existed, they resolved, and at once, to meet the calamity with fortitude, and to remedy it. . . .

"The greatest misfortunes often bring a breath of consolation on their wings. So of this dreadful conflagration. The city had been crowded with goods. The enormous profits which the adventurers had realized had induced many others to make large shipments. Thus a vast amount of goods filled the stores and storehouses, and the market was, as a natural consequence, dormant and ruinous. The fire came and furnished a market for a great portion of the stock, and although the returns for it made no very flattering balance in the ledger, still the enhanced value of what remained partially compensated for what had been lost. Consequently, business soon revived.

"Within ten days, between two and three hundred buildings had been completed, or were in a fair state of progression, within the burnt district. About fifteen hundred buildings had been destroyed within ten hours. At nine o'clock, on the morning of May 4th, the last of that number was a bed of ruins; but, by the 14th of the same month, fully one-fifth of the whole number destroyed was again fit for habitation and business, or were fast approaching that condition. Such determination, energy and perseverance soon swept out nearly all traces of the fire from the face of the city. And people with buoyant hearts hoped and trusted that the city had passed through her last great affliction. But another trial still awaited her and them. Still another fire anniversary approached. The 14th of June of the previous year had been signalized by a very disastrous conflagration, and the citizens feared a repetition of the frightful anniversary of the 4th of the preceding May.

"Again it was whispered that the lawless gang of desperadoes who still infested the city had threatened to keep the anniversary of the fire of June 14th, 1850, in a manner suitable to the scenes of that day, and their own sentiments of hatred and revenge. Two days before, one of their number — Jenkins — had been hanged on the plaza by the enraged populace; and that class of villains to which he belonged, it was said, had sworn vengeance. But great vigilance prevented the consummation of the fiendish attempt, if such was intended. However, this state of security was not to last long. Sunday, June 22nd, came, with its winning call to peace, quiet and devotion. The bells were ringing out their invitation to prayer and praise, and the streets were filled with people on their way to public worship. Just then the bells changed their tone, and terror succeeded all feelings of devotion. The *sixth* great fire had commenced, and the buildings of nearly fifteen squares had felt the sun's light for the last time. People forgot the church and rushed to the scene of conflagration on the corner of Pacific and Powell streets. The prayer-book, the altar and the Bible, psalm, hymn and sermon, passed by unheeded, and the dreaded devastator's court took precedence of pew and pulpit, prayer and exhortation. An immense crowd was at once at the scene of disaster. The firemen were there, too, but no reservoirs were near, and the element had its will. Like Hercules it rose superior to all opposition. The flames were too rapid, and the heat in a short time became so intense that every person was driven from the vicinity. Buildings were blown up, but that availed nothing. The shattered wreck was soon in a blaze, and burned with all the more intensity. Men contended with the flames until they could not breathe, and then left their offices and dwellings, and rushed into the streets, or upon the plaza. There, most melancholy sights met the view. Large portions of the goods removed there for safety, caught fire and were totally consumed. But the most horrible sight of all was that of two or three corpses, one of a man who, being sick, was removed in his bed to the plaza, and there died while the fire was raging. Another was the trunk of a man burned to death, and partly consumed. The scene here was singular and terrific. Goods had been moved to it from all parts of the city, but they caught fire from the intense heat and cinders, and a third part of them was destroyed. Patients from the hospital, women and children, were gathered there, or hurried thence as from certain destruction. . . ."

Disaster in April

The earthquake and fire that was to be San Francisco's last great catastrophe came about 5 o'clock on the morning of April 18, 1906. The whole city creaked, trembled and shook violently, settling to periodic jolts and tremors for several minutes. Building walls collapsed, houses tilted and crumbled, streets buckled and flames sprang up in the most heavily populated areas of the business district. Water mains burst and firemen were all but helpless.

The city was put under martial law and explosions alternated with the crack and crash of falling masonry as buildings were dynamited to prevent the spread of fire. By noon the whole town was in flight, to the Oakland and Alameda ferries, to Golden Gate Park—a mass migration of refugees with carts, baby carriages, toy wagons piled with hastily salvaged possessions. On the streets up the slopes men and women cooked on improvised stoves, offering coffee and food to the perplexed and frightened. On Nob Hill the wealthy were taking everyone and anyone into their stately mansions if they were left standing.

The fire raged all day and into the night of the 19th when it was stopped at Van Ness Avenue. Ten square miles lay in ruins and half of San Francisco was homeless . . . but in the midst of destruction relief and rebuilding had started.

(Below, left) CALIFORNIA STREET buckles as fire is watched by stoical Chinese. (Opposite, top) Smoke of controlled explosions is added to that of fire. (Below, right) Market Street, looking through desolation of April 18, 1906, toward Ferry Building.

(Above left) FIREMEN spray burning homes with little hope of checking flames. (Center) Police patrol ruins on Montgomery St. south of Market. (Right) Grant Ave. from Market St. 4 days after earthquake and fires.

(Below) GRANT AVENUE on morning of April 19, 1906. (Opposite, bottom) Fire started in various areas, could not be controlled when water mains broke.

(Above, left) GOTHIC ARCH of wrecked telephone building forms interpretive backdrop for army relief tent. (Above center) Clearing up debris after April 18 fire.

(Left) NOB HILL RUIN of "gold fortune" mansion.

(Above, right) SMILES AND ANTICS for photographer as city flames and fumes. (Right) Tenants have fled "leaning towers" on Sutter Street.

MINING TOWN of Mercur burning June 26, 1902.

UTAH *"From the hoist house I could see the flames . . ."*

said volunteer fireman William Waterfall of Mercur, Utah.

"I was operating the electrical hoist for the Consolidated Mercur Mines, which raised and lowered workmen to and from the mine and to different levels. The cage was about 1,500 feet away from the operator when the the phone rang. I answered and was told that a serious fire had broken out down town. From outside the hoist house I could see the flames coming through the roof of the Preble Building. I blew the fire signal and phoned the mine, telling them to turn out as the town was doomed. By the time I reached town, 1,200 feet below the hoist house, the fire was beyond control. By 12 o'clock every business house in the town was gone."

This account written from "The Ghost of Mercur" by Douglas D. Alder appearing in "Utah Historical Quarterly" of January 1961.

Today a jumble of rusty pipes and cement tanks filled with sediment listens to the lazy tinkle of sheep bells and remembers the lively mining town of the early 1900s.

An ore discovery was made here in 1879 by Arie Pinedo who thought the vein was cinnabar and being a Bavarian, he named the lode "der Merkur." Gold was turned up in 1883 but not until the '90s was it mined in quantity. In 1899 several interests joined to form the Consolidated Mercur Gold Mines Co. which prospered and kept the town alive until 1917. The fire on June 26, 1902, described by volunteer fireman Waterfall, leveled the entire business district but did not reach the mill which continued to operate until 1913.

(Opposite) BUSINESS DISTRICT of Mercur, Utah, before disastrous fire of June 26, 1902. Scene is likely 4th of July celebration.

(Above) GOLDEN GATE MILL at end of street dominates town of Mercur, July 4, 1901, year before big fire. (Below) Mill now looks down on devastated Mercur 2½ hours after fire started. Shell of brick building is one shown above behind bandstand.

8 · 9 · 10 · 11 · 12 · '13 'Chief'

(Above, center) MERCUR FIRE DEPARTMENT volunteers one year after June 26, 1902 fire. (Above, right) New city hall and fire-fighting crew July 4, 1903. (Bottom) View of Mercur ruins up canyon to left of street shown opposite.

"NOT WITHOUT DUST AND HEAT." The hiss and crackle of flames in dry wood, the shouts of "Jump her, boys!" as firemen leap to the roofs, the burned-out citizens staring in wide-eyed and open-mouthed panic . . . all the drama of the early-day fire is shown in this Bingham Canyon, Utah, fire at Highland Boy — Sept. 8, 1932.

Fire Bell in the Night

Someone in Helena, Montana, once said, "A fire in these diggings is just one Chinaman away." Wherever you had flimsy buildings in narrow, windy gulches, not much water and too many Chinamen, the danger of fire was ever present. The watchword was, "Don't throw matches in a pile of straw," but Chinamen didn't understand English or watchwords very well.

All gold camps in the west had destructive fires but most of them were too busy living on the edge of prosperity to do much more than build new shacks to feed the next fire. Helena was lucky to grow into a town and have citizens who got tired of being routed out of bed at 2 a.m. because somebody took a coal oil lantern into the barn and dropped it when the cow went "Moo." So the town installed an iron triangle on a hill and at the first wisp of alien smoke a watchman would beat the alarm and people would grab the water buckets hanging on the walls and run to help put the fire out, hoping there was water handy.

After the big fire of 1870, watchman Carl Miller tried to get an extra key to the Methodist Church which had a new bell so he could sound a louder alarm, but says the legend, the church elders either suspected him of being a Baptist or the representative of a fire bell syndicate and turned their attentions, along with those of the town officials, to getting a new fire engine, hook and ladders, ropes, more buckets and axes. It was not until after more bad fires, especially the one in 1874, that a bell was obtained and a tower built for it on the hill.

In 1886 a larger bell was installed. It cost $525 and weighed 2,200 pounds. It was made of copper, East India mallora and block tin. When the bell tower was strengthened to support it, a room was built for the watchman, with glass on four sides, where he could swivel around in a chair like a bank president, watch for smoke in the wrong places and think profound thoughts such as the un-Methodist ones his predecessor, Carl Miller, probably had.

MONTANA *Helena swept by costly blaze . . . 1872*

Under the headline, "Another Devastating Conflagration," the Helena, Montana, *Daily Herald* of August 24, 1872, gave stirring details of the fire that destroyed more than 60 buildings in the mining center the previous day, the fourth crippling fire in the town's short history.

"Helena has again been swept by a destructive conflagration. Yesterday, F r i d a y, August 23, about 3 o'clock p.m. an incipient fire was discovered in the rear part of the North Pacific Hotel on Main Street, below Broadway. The alarm was immediately given by citizens in the vicinity, and taken up by the watchman in the fire tower and sounded over the city. Multitudes of people hurriedly gathered from all parts of the metropolis, and with buckets, hose, axes, tackle, and such other articles and implements as were useful and to be had, commenced a prompt and vigorous fight with the Fire Fiend. But small and seemingly insignificant puffs of smoke were first observable issuing from the roof above the kitchen range. Numbers of men, conspicuously active and efficient on all occasions of similar danger— whose names are known and whose services are recognized by all our people—precipitated themselves upon the building, and with axes and water buckets endeavored to reach and extinguish the smouldering fire. Their efforts, however, proved unavailing; the pent-up fire speedily burst forth in a n g r y blaze and wrapped the roof in an extended sheet of flame. Driven from the hotel top, the corps of "fire fighters" retired to the roofs of contiguous buildings, and, assisted by large numbers of citizen workers, commenced a rapid demolition of the temporary board and shingle coverings of adjoining fireproof business houses. But a few m i n u t e s transpired before the North Pacific, (a vast tinder box in itself) and frame building adjoining, occupied by the junior Holter as a saloon, were enveloped in lurid flame and produced an intense heat. The wooden covers above the fireproofs of Murphy, Neal & Co., Hall & Hagedorn, on the one side, and of J. H. Curtis on the other, were removed, but the conflagration had too great a mass to work on to successfully cope with it, and the fire wound around the rear of Taylor's stone block, and fastened itself upon the frame building corner of Main Street and Broadway, occupied as a grocery house by Hall & Hagedorn. This speedily went down, but not until most of the merchandise had been got out or safely stored in the rear fireproof. But a moment later the whirling firebrands, communicating with the residence of Mr. G. S. Ellis, immediately back and across Jackson Street, set that building ablaze as also the extensive carpenter shop of Ellis Bros. adjoining, destroying edifices, furniture, tools, machinery, and lumber in frightful haste. The wind, blowing strong from the west, veered to southwest and back again, sweeping the fire straight ahead, and right and left to Broadway and Grand Street.

"Human effort seemed utterly impotent to stay the ravages of the inexorable demon, enfolding in fiery embrace many a structure and swiftly spreading over a goodly portion of the business and residence portion of the city. Simultaneously, the elegant new cottage-house of Rev. Dr. Curtiss and the residence of Mr. Rae, on Grand Street, and the frame business houses on Broadway above Jackson, took fire and were enveloped in the furious flame. The *Gazette* office, located in the stone building on Jackson Street, was sandwiched between burning buildings, but it was thought that the thick walls and cement roof would save the house and contents. Not until the imposing Whitlatch block, corner of Broadway and Jackson, took fire and got under full headway, was the *Gazette* establishment deemed in imminent danger. . . .

"The new Methodist Church South, corner of Grand and Warren Streets, was several times on fire, but was promptly extinguished by courageous men, who worked themselves to the lofty roof and deluged the smoking shingles with buckets of water. . . . The fire had spent its fury only upon reaching Court House Square, and the blowing up and razing to the ground of log and frame buildings facing the square alone sufficed to save the public buildings, including the court house, county jail, etc., as well as the adjacent residences fronting Breckenridge Street on the north. . . ."

(Above and right) HELENA, MONTANA, suffered its fourth serious fire on August 23, 1874, when strong wind whipped destruction over seven blocks in central business and residence area.

FLIMSY SHACKS burn with swift, hot fury in Dawson, Yukon Territory, April 26, 1899.

PHOTO BY F.H. NOWELL

ALASKA . . . YUKON TERRITORY

1977

THE RUINS OF THE BANK OF BRITISH NORTH AMERICA
APRIL 26th 99   DAWSON Y.T

(Above) RUINS OF BANK of British North America in Dawson's 1899 fire. (Right) Fire in Nome Sept. 13, 1905.

VIRGINIA M. TUTT BRANCH
2002 Miami Street
South Bend, Indiana 46613

NOME, ALASKA, had first fire May 25, 1901.

BRITISH COLUMBIA

OPERA HOUSE at Nelson, British Columbia, going up in flames.

On the heels of a coal mine explosion on July 29, 1908, fire came roaring out of the timber with tornadolike force to sweep Fernie, British Columbia, away in 90 minutes. The explosion took more lives, the "bump" entombing fifty miners, but the fire took Fernie.

Forest fires plagued Elk Valley all that summer and people were so used to the smoke-saturated air they thought little of it on the hot morning of July 30. But the woods crew of the Elk Valley Lumber Co. did. Their camp shut down and instead of setting chokers the men were set to forming a fire line so that the light wind would not blow the fire into more timber and the town.

But the fire had its own ideas and created its own wind, a much stronger one, whushing into the crowns of the trees over the loggers' heads, forcing them to the safety of a sandbar in Elk River. And that was the end of the sawmill. The flames roared out of the timber, ate up the mill and 20 million feet of lumber in a raging inferno, the force of it so great it blew burning planks and timbers into the air and sent showers of glowing debris into Fernie. The fire bell clanged but citizens did not need that to tell them there was big trouble. They groped their way through the acrid murk on the streets and hurried to their homes and stores to save what they could.

The volunteer fire brigade tried to stop the march of the fire at the Fernie-Fort Steele Brewery while hundreds of West Fernians were running over the Great Northern Railway trestle to the east bank of the river. The brewery was lost, the singed and smudged fire fighters retreating into the town to make another stand.

It was panic and pandemonium with the townspeople — men and women dragging children and baggage, fleeing their lives in a wild scramble, many of the helpless screaming to be saved. "A man on a horse couldn't keep ahead of that fire," said Mayor "Bill" Tuttle. The wind and vacuum created by the leaping flames pulled trees up by their roots and hurled men against walls. The roof of the skating rink blew off and up, crashing in flaming splinters against buildings blocks away. The

(Above) FERNIE, British Columbia, in Elk Valley coal field after fire of Aug. 1, 1908. (Bottom, opposite) Ruins of Victoria Ave., Fernie, British Columbia.

Waldorf Hotel collapsed and sent sheets of fire down the street.

A train was quickly made up at the depot and terrified citizens pulled and clawed through the crowds to climb aboard, swarming over the engine and tender. Underway, it roared over a burning trestle toward Hosmer while hundreds, not being able to ride, threw themselves into gullies and ditches full of hot water. Some were scorched or almost boiled, one family seeking refuge in a well and all were suffocated.

The train thundered into the forest between walls of blazing trees, passengers in the exposed vestibules burned by the showers of sparks, the ones inside behind closed windows baked in the awful heat, screaming as the flames flashed at the glass. And passing through Hosmer the train was bombarded by

a hail of dirt and rocks as a powder house exploded. Beyond the town and danger, the refugees were turned loose and the engineer took the train back to Fernie for more human freight to find a CPR engine pulling out with a string of boxcars loaded with humans and headed for Kingsgate.

In the 90 minutes it took the fire to sweep through Fernie, hot ashes had replaced homes and business establishments, 1,200 buildings were g o n e with the fiery wind, 6,000 people were homeless and seven were dead. Gone were the town's two newspapers, opera house, new courthouse, new post office, banks, schools and churches. The CPR loss approached $500,000 which included the station and miles of twisted rails. The Great Northern lost its depot, freight sheds, trestles, bridges and 200 boxcars loaded with coke and coal. Even steel cars were buckled and warped into useless scrap.

Nurses, relief workers, and a telegraph operator worked heroically and Mayor Tuttle sent a message to Cranbrook summing up the damage and asking for bread and tents. Citizens there had just finished a three days' fight against fire in their own area but sent a trainload of supplies immediately.

Another message to Spokane brought more relief goods — 2,000 loaves of bread, 50 barrels of flour, meat, canned milk, tea, coffee, sugar, bedding and tents. As the train crossed the border, it whistled for the inspection stop but customs agents waved it on through. A Spokane trucking firm sent horses and trucks to the beleaguered Fernie.

Mayor Tuttle and committees organized clean-up and relief work. Supplies were unloaded, tents pitched and workers at once began dispensing food, clothing, shoes and medical supplies. Women fell to washing dishes and children. Rev. Hugh Grant had helpers finding misplaced children and families, sending wires and letters to relatives of those burned out. Chief of Police Bob Clark and provincial constables swore in dozens of deputies and, although both city and provincial police stations were burned out, officers prevented any mob violence and looting. There were no liquor stocks left after the fire to complicate police work and officials allowed none to enter the distressed area.

Jack McDonald, secretary of the United Mine Workers union, received relief funds from other locals and newspapers were able to print again when type and a press were dispatched from Winnipeg. General relief funds came piling in from towns on both sides of the border, totaling some $120,000. Insurance companies reported a staggering loss in claims amounting to two and a half million dollars. And all this damage was done in a 90-minute holocaust.

(Above, left) AFTER FERNIE
FIRE. Victoria Avenue opposite
Bank of Commerce. (Center)
Relief headquarters and (right)
weighing meat for relief supplies.

(Right) REFUGEES' "HOMES"
and (below) West Fernie starting to build up.

SOME FERNIE FIRE "REFUGEES"

(Above) BURNED-OUT citizens of Fernie "re-
fueling" on emergency rations.

(Below) THEY LOST everything but good humor
in Fernie fire of 1908.

YALE, BRITISH COLUMBIA, on day following July 1880 fire.

A third of Yale was in ashes... 1880

"A Sunday in Yale . . . presented a scene at once grotesque, bizarre, risque," wrote a miner on his way up the Fraser River to the Cariboo gold country. "The one long street fronted on the river . . . shell-like shacks of saloons whereof every third building was one, fairly buzzed and bulged like Brobdignagian wasps' nests, whose inmates in a continuous state of flux, ever and anon hurled in and out in twos and threes, or tangled mingling masses. Painted and bedizened women lent a garish color to the scene. On the hot and dusty roadside or around piles of timbers, rails or other R.R. construction debris, men in advanced stages of intoxi-

cation rolled or fought or snored in bestial oblivion."

In July 1880, a third of the town of 1,500 inhabitants, the "wildest place on the West Coast in that day," was destroyed by fire. All the buildings were of wood and burned like matchboxes, sending miners, gamblers and fancy ladies out into the dusty street "whooping and hollering." One saloonkeeper set up a tent and handed out free drinks to the burned-out citizens, the number of whom suddenly increased at the gesture. The next day shacks were slapped together over the cold ashes and in a week Yale was her wild and woolly self.

SPOKANE STREET, Rossland, British Columbia, ablaze in afternoon of August 25, 1902.

Rossland had historic fire in 1902

At 3 p.m. on August 25, 1902, just before the change of shift in the mines, fire broke out in Burns and Company's store in Spokane Street. The employees herded everyone outside but the fire swept around First Avenue corner stores which burned like kindling. An hour later the Trail fire brigade arrived by special train.

By 5 o'clock the main course of the fire had been checked but the huge International Hotel was consumed entirely as were all buildings on blocks west and north of the fire's origin. Chief D. Guthrie was trapped on the second floor of the Burns Building. As he jumped, his legs caught on power wires and he was knocked unconscious as he struck the ground, later recovering in a hospital.

(Left) ROSSLAND, British Columbia, in 1902. (Opposite, top) Rossland fire from Earl Street on top of cliff. (Opposite, bottom) Firemen battle blaze at southeast corner of First Avenue. Big International Hotel was saved.

Barkerville in smouldering ruins . . . 1868

Sparks on a dry roof ignited a blaze that developed into a roaring furnace "hot enough to melt the gold right out of the veins" in the Cariboo mining town of Barkerville. Six days later, Sept. 22, 1868, the Cariboo *Sentinel* told the story and took a penetrating look at the losses in the "BURNING OF BARKER-VILLE."

"Long ere this the news of the conflagration of the town of Barkerville, Williams Creek, has flashed across the wires to all parts of the civilized world. It remains only for us to give in detail an account of the circumstances and results connected therewith. No one but an eyewitness can form any correct conception of a scene so fraught with disastrous results — of a momentary character at least — for we do not apprehend that the calamity, although universal as far as the town of Barkerville is concerned, is one that to any material extent will retard the general prospects of the country or the permanent mining interests in Cariboo. Only a few days since we, with much pride, spoke of the order and neatness here and our ink had scarcely dried ere the town was a mass of smouldering ruins, and charred timbers and heaps of rubbish only marked the spot where stood the metropolis of Cariboo. In just one hour the merciless element had turned the tenants of 120 houses roofless into the streets, and many with no more property than covered their persons.

"The fire first made its appearance in the roof of Adler & Barry's saloon near the centre of the town, at half past 2 o'clock p.m. on Wednesday, the 16th inst. The alarm was instantly carried to all parts of the town but a single glance seemed sufficient to convince everyone that to attempt to extinguish the flames was useless, consequently each one turned his at-

BARKERVILLE, famous gold camp in Cariboo country of British Columbia, before 1868 fire.

tention to the rescue of his own property. Those whose houses were somewhat remote had a fair chance of saving most of their property, but those more contiguous had no chance whatever, owing to the character of the buildings, which were all of light material and very dry. The flames spread in all directions with great rapidity, and after one or two faint and unsuccessful attempts to check its progress, the town was abandoned to its fate, except near the extreme ends. At the upper end, at Scott's saloon, where the Barker ditch crossed the street in a flume, the fire was checked for some time and had there been any degree of organization or concert of action it could have here been stopped, and Strauss' store, containing the largest stock of goods in the town, might have been saved. Scott's saloon only was saved, which is attributed to the ready supply of water from the ditch, of which Scott, an old and skillful fireman, knew how to avail himself. Here the fire parted and swept past through Chinatown and exhausted itself for want of further prey. The effort at the lower end of town was a little more successful. The progress of the flames was stopped just before it reached McInnes' saloon, which was saved, and also the warehouse of I. Weill and the H. B. Co. In just one hour and twenty minutes from the first cry of fire and the last roof fell, and the destruction of Barkerville was pronounced complete, and fleeing hundreds, with goods snatched from the flames, with relaxed limbs sat down upon their rescued plunder, and with long-drawn breath wiped the perspiration from their brows. . . .

"Soon after the fire abated, the despoiled merchants commenced to gather in their goods which were rescued from the flames and it soon became apparent that thieves had been in the field, for large quantities known to have been saved were missing. Search was immediately commenced and continued throughout the night and the following day, and many thousand dollars worth were found concealed in cabins and old shafts, and on various trails leading from the town; but notwithstanding so much has been rescued, it is still believed that a large quantity of stolen goods is yet undiscovered. . . .

"There probably never was a conflagration of such magnitude, or so destructive to property, in which so few accidents occurred to the person as in the present case. Not a single life was lost, nor a personal injury sustained worthy of note. The only alarming incident was the temporary prostration of Mr. H. S. Blunt, the manager of the Bank of British Columbia, who from overexertion and extreme exhaustion, after saving all the treasure and books of the Bank, fell into a spasmodic fit, from the effects of which he has recovered.

"Much comment is made upon the conduct of the people during the fire, in regard to their attempts, or rather non-attempts to stop the progress thereof. In the absence of any regularly organized fire company, the first duty of the people is to submit to a voluntary organization pro tem, and had this rule been observed, we have no doubt that the fire could have been suppressed at a much earlier period. We have seen impromptu organizations of this kind in country towns where no fire company existed, suppress fires of greater magnitude than the present one; but the population in such cases was one of more permanent character, and such concentrated efforts had become to them a custom. Had the same disposition and readiness for combined action characterized the people of Barkerville, we do not doubt that the greater portion of the town could have been saved. We do not wish, however, to speak reproachfully of the conduct of anyone, as all, no doubt, acted as they thought most prudent. . . . Whether the saying, 'experience teaches fools' be true or false, the probability is that in the future history of Barkerville it will be found that those who invest their entire fortune in wooden buildings will be more careful in guarding against a similar contingency by taking the proper means for protection. . . .

"No ordinary pen sketch can convey a true conception of the scene which followed the fire. Night was drawing on and hundreds of men, women and children were compelled to seek shelter, and tons of goods and chattels lay scattered along the creek and on the hillsides; and like ants whose storehouses had been overturned by the plowshare, the despoiled human swarm were seen running in every direction, loaded with their wares, seeking a place of refuge. Women and children with beds, pots and pans, and men with huge packages of bacon, or sacks of flour and beans, tugging away to a place of shelter; whilst here and there might be seen someone whose courage was not of the sterling type, giving way to lamentations and tears; but upon the whole there probably never was a calamity so sudden or complete more heroically or philosophically bourne. . . ."

(Right) DETAIL OF BARKER-VILLE buildings destroyed as shown in photo below.

"Black Day" in British Columbia's "Royal City"

"The sky itself seemed to be on fire," said one citizen of New Westminster as the city burned that night, Sept. 10, 1898. And when the last flame died, hundreds were homeless and the business district devastated.

Sometime in the late evening of that Saturday a fire was detected in a store of hay on on the Brackman & Ker dock on the Frazer River. About 11 p.m. firemen answered the alarm and found flames leaping wildly before the wind and could make little headway against the intense heat as the fire engulfed the whole warehouse, jumped Front Street to set fire to the Lytton Hotel and business buildings.

It was still a fire that could be controlled, said Acting Fire Chief Watson, had two boats not been tied up at the burning wharf. As the flames ate it up, they reached the *Gladys* and *Edgar,* burned up the mooring lines and the craft, like Roman funeral pyres, went adrift and set fire to every dock they touched.

The entire waterfront was now a raging holocaust, C. P. Navigation wharf ablaze, the *Bon Accord* another firey torch afloat which in turn fired a coal-carrying scow. To save a cannery ship from burning, it was sunk but the Sinclair & Western Fisheries cannery was belching fire, clouds of sparks and shingles into the red smoke blanketing the city. Then the fire hose burned through and Vancouver was called for help and replacements.

Chinatown was burning, people were fleeing from the houses below Agnes Street and the streets leading up the hill were blocked by wagons, carts and heaps of household goods. The *Columbian* office, Y.M.C.A., public library, Bank of British Columbia and No. 1 Fire Hall were going fast. When water pressure sagged, the New Westminster and Vancouver firemen used pressure from a river steamer and prevented further damage beyond 10th Street. They fought the fire until 5 a.m. and dawn saw 60 blocks of business and residential properties destroyed and losses to $2½ million.

COLUMBIA STREET in New Westminster after fire of Sept. 10, 1898 consumed entire business district and many homes.

(Above) TEMPORARY QUAR-
TERS are put together quickly
as city sorts itself out of ashes.
(Right) Ruins of public buildings and (b e l o w) Columbia
Street on Sept. 11, 1898, day after
fire.

(Opposite) BUSINESS BLOCKS
and public buildings, New Westminster, after devastating fire.

Vancouver citizens flee burning city . . . 1886

"Fire" was the black, blunt headline in the Vancouver Weekly *Herald* of Friday, June 18, 1886, over the glowing words of calamity in the six-month-old city.

"The morning of Sunday, the 13th inst.," said the writer, "opened calm, bright and beautiful over the new and growing city of Vancouver; the sun set calm and beautiful over the blackened ruins of that young city. No one on the morning of that fatal day dreamt that such a terrible calamity would befall them. Many, induced by the fine, bright weather, had gone on boating excursions, others had betaken themselves to the many quiet and beautiful nooks that surround the city to, enjoy undisturbed the beautiful scenery, and learn a sermon from Nature's tongue that mortal could not impart, and many were enjoying that quietude and happiness of the family circle, which the Sabbath alone brought them, all unconscious of the fearful fiend that would ravage and devastate the city. Many went to church and took part in the worship of God, never for an instant thinking that the walls which surrounded them and the roof which covered them would be a heap of ruins at sunset. . . .

"About 8 o'clock when a slight breeze sprung up from the southwest; it increased towards 10 o'clock, and the smoke from the fires in the clearing grew denser, hanging over the city like a vast funeral pall. No one, however, appeared to apprehend danger and took no notice of the progress the fire was making. Not till about two o'clock in the afternoon did it seem to cause any harm, and even then when those who saw the danger spoke of it, it was disbelieved by many. About 2:30 people in the West end of the city began taking out their goods and chattles; but before they had time to attempt their removal the fire caught one of the buildings on Water Street, and the wind having increased to a gale, swept it along with astounding rapidity. The citizens were thrown into confusion, and many panic-striken with the sudden outbreak, ran in every direction seeking safety from the destroyer. Some ran into the water and took to boats, canoes or anything that was afloat, others ran towards False Creek and many to the Hastings' Mill. Half an hour from the time the first building caught fire the devouring flames had swept along the whole length of Water Street, at the same time destroying everything between the Royal City Planing Mills Company's saw mill

VANCOUVER, BRITISH COLUMBIA, after fire that wiped out six-week city on June 13, 1886.

REFUGEES' BIVOUAC on morning after Vancouver burned, June 13, 1886.

and warehouses on False Creek (which were saved) and the waters of the Inlet. Leaping across Carroll Street, Mr. Ferguson's fine building was the next victim to the insatiable fiend, and eased not until it had swept everything to the Eastern boundary of the eighty-five acre tract and south to Keefer Street, taking also the residences of the Rev. Mr. Thomson and Mr. Soule between Mr. R. H. Alexander's residence and that of Mr. Coldwell, and within 150 yards of the Hastings Saw Mill Company's wharf. In forty-five minutes from the time the fire caught the first building it had swept over the whole city, leaving nothing behind it but heaps of debris. At the Hastings Saw Mill wharf the scene was heartrending, children crying for their mothers, mothers for their children, wives for their husbands, and husbands for their wives. Capt. Rogers, of the steamer *Robert Dunsmuir*, when the fire was first reported to him immediately caused the fires to be lit and steam got up as quickly as possible. About 250 persons had taken refuge on board his steamer, and he conveyed them across the Inlet to Moodyville to pass the night. . . .

"Several narrow escapes are reported, but no creditable information can be had of them yet. One was reported to us by the parties themselves. Messrs. J. Boultbee and C. G. Johnson had a severe scorching. They were trying to reach False Creek bridge and the fire overtook them. Fortunately they got to a lot which had been cleared, they each dug a hole in the ground, bade each other goodbye, and lay down flat with their heads in the holes. They lay there for about an hour suffering very acutely. Eight bodies have been recovered . . .

"Over 2500 were rendered homeless, many without a change of clothing, and many without a cent in their possession. Many who were in comfortable circumstances in a few hours were rendered destitute, depending for the means of sustenance on the charity of others. All were sufferers in a greater or lesser degree, not one escaped without experiencing a loss of some kind. . . ."

95

(Above) HASTINGS MILL, historic landmark in panorama of Vancouver, British Columbia, before the fire, 1886. Many people fled to safety here during fire.

(Below) VANCOUVER from area burned out in 1886. Flags are across Cordova Street at first CPR office, foot of Seymour.

Armstrong suffered worst fire in 1901

ARMSTRONG before and after devastation in early morning hours of Aug. 10, 1901. In one hour 16 business structures lay in smouldering ruins as result of fire set by demented resident named Eagles, "to get even with a lot of people who were trying to poison me."

Carey Castle, Victoria, destroyed by fire

All night fire smouldered in the attic of Carey Castle, picturesque and historic residence of the Lieutenant-Governor of the Province. In the early morning of May 18, 1899, it burst forth and destroyed the whole building except ballroom and conservatory.

Private secretary T. R. E. McInnes discovered the blaze. He was on his way to breakfast and heard a crackling noise as though the whole roof were on fire. Running a gauntlet of falling embers, he gave the alarm.

The Lieutenant-Governor and family saved what possessions they could but most of the upper portion of the building was enveloped in flames and they could move articles from only the main floor. With the exception of his uniform which was taken out when the alarm was first sounded, the family lost all personal effects, including clothing, jewelry and private papers.

The "castle" was called by many "an architectural freak." It was built in 1859 by G. H. Carey, attorney general of the colony, at a cost of $30,000 to replace the original Carey House erected the year previous which was also claimed by fire.

(Above and below) EARLY LANDMARK in Victoria — Old Government House called "Carey's Folly" — was destroyed by fire May 18, 1899. "Castle" was architectural freak, built in 1858 as original residence of G. H. Carey, attorney general of colony.

SACRAMENTO steam engine of Rainier Valley Fire Department, Georgetown, rival city of Seattle —one of earliest pumpers in use on Pacific Coast.

Pumpers and Pride

When the "cider mill" and "coffee grinder" began pulling water out of ditches and cisterns and shooting streams of water forty feet, the machine age was warning volunteer firemen it was on its way. In a few years they would be selling pencils on the corners and cadging drinks in saloons while paid professionals took over their work with even bigger and better engines. Only the machine age did not say that. It said, with a carefully concealed sneer, "Boys, the towns are getting too big for the crude methods you've been using. Look at these beautiful, modern, efficient machines. They will give your outfits a chance to put out some fires and your chests a chance to wear some medals."

The gooseneck machines did look beautiful and the volunteer firemen considered themselves pretty lucky when their towns took tax funds or public subscription money and bought a pumper or maybe two, even established added fire companies. The firemen responded by buying bright, bold uniforms and new hats with silver badges on them because the fire companies were civic opportunities and it was a mark of distinction to belong to them, a rare privilege that made even dull men the center of attention. This new status recharted the lives of willing adherents. They spent more and more time polishing machine brass and often neglected to polish their own. They attended engine company meetings and fire drills, played baseball against other companies and competed in races and hose-laying contests, strutted in fancy dress at town socials and balls . . . well, who needed a business or job, anyhow? This was the life of Riley.

The mechanical marvels which the firemen petted, pampered and pumped were, without doubt, things of beauty and proper joys until a fire broke out. Then it was jumping to the harness and hauling the heavy rigs to the fires, laying hose to the water — or another engine to increase the pressure — and putting six to twelve men on every set of brakes to pump their eyeballs out while the heat blistered the slick red paint and

99

scorched the leather hose. Even with machines, this was putting out fires the hard way.

Yet it did put them out, at least some of them. Frank Soule, in his *Annals of San Francisco,* wrote of the year 1852: "No one any longer apprehends any danger from fire in San Francisco. With fifty large public cisterns already constructed, others under way, and numerous others built by private individuals; with thirteen powerful and well-supplied engines, and three hook and ladder companies, under the control of an average of nine hundred and fifty certificate members (who are by statute exempt from jury duty while members, and after five years' service, exempt for life), the most dangerous fire can be subdued."

Apparatus used in San Francisco and other progressive western communities in the 1850s to 1870s included side-lever engines, piano boxes, goose-neck types, end stroke and side stroke pumpers, the "cider mill' and "coffee grinder." The goose-neck fire engine was so called from the curl of the eduction pipe which extended up from the air chamber. The "coffee grinder" was a rotary type operated by a crank on each side, handles accommodating six or eight men. The "cider mill" claimed great suction power with a rotary pump worked like a ship's capstan, firemen pushing the bars by walking around the engines.

William C. Hunneman, an apprentice of Paul Revere, and Ephriam Thayer developed end stroke engines which were in popular use on the West Coast. These operated with the brakes on balance beams or rocker arms and used up to eight men on each set of brakes. The Philadelphia-type engines had double banks of brakes at each end as did the Shanghai-type.

The side stroke piano or piano-box engine had 7" cylinders and 5" stroke. The suction hose was attached to the rear and when not in use was swung up over the top and held in place by a large brass pipe. So equipped, the engines were dubbed "Squirrel Tails." The walking beams or crossarms of the pumping mechanism were slotted so the leverage could be altered without changing the length of stroke. When in operation, brakes could be lowered from folded position to breast-high pumping position.

The crane-neck or piano crane-neck engine was a larger side stroke type as was the Carson piano type. A side stroke engine known as the "Haywagon" because of a rick-like set of double brakes was also in use in the West. It was also called "Mankiller," being especially heavy and hard to pump, but likewise was very powerful with 9½" cylinders and 9" stroke, playing a stream of water higher and farther than most other engines of the period.

Hand engines were normally operated at about sixty strokes a minute, sometimes speeded up to double this tempo. A stroke consisted of a full up and down motion of the brakes and, at normal paces, a man could last at this pumping about ten minutes, less if the speed was very great. Firemen frequently suffered from torn fingers and broken arms sustained when jumping in as relief when an engine was being operated at high speed.

The pride firemen took in their engines extended to decorating them almost to the point of art, the work done on their off-duty time and at their own expense. They gave machines pet names and much paint, using gold leaf and adding burnished brass fittings freely. Engines with large boxes having spacious panel areas were often decorated with paintings or designs and running gear was gaily striped, gilded or silvered. Mottoes such as "Duty Our Pleasure" or "Ever Ready, Ever Willing" were lettered or worked out in wrought iron. Some companies made the panels of their engines removable so the workaday wear and tear, heat, smoke and water at fires would not mar their works of art.

And Sunday morning was the time for keeping all this beauty spick and span. As many of the men as possible gathered at the station. Nickel and brass pipes and fittings were polished, leather casings and covers dressed, machinery and wheels greased, ropes recoiled. Bills, hooks, pikes and axes were ground, cleaned and oiled. Signal lamps and torches were scoured and filled with fuel. Tools were checked, hose spanners, half-spanners and wrenches placed in proper place. And standing back in loving contemplation the men would say, "Nobody is going to come along and say our Dollie Dimple is being neglected!"

In its issue of March 9, 1882, the *Fireman's Herald* sang the sweet story in verse:

"Behold! How she shines in her beauty,
    Resplendent in silver and gold;
Ne'er shrinking from doing her duty,
    When worked by her members so bold;
So peacefully innocent standing,
    You'd dream not the work she can do,
But when we her aid are demanding,
    She always proves faithful and true."

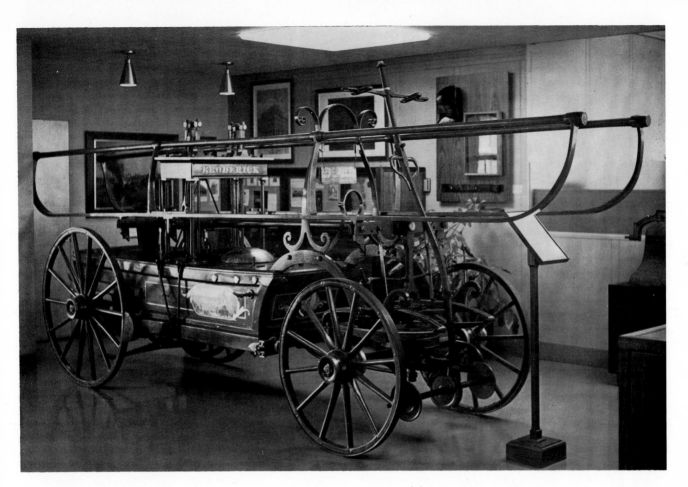

Museum piece once used with "pomp and parade"

The handsome, side-stroke veteran of San Francisco's volunteer firemen days, its brass polished and red paint gleaming, was considered the first fire engine built in the state of California — its name, Broderick No. 1. Found discarded in a Kelowna, B.C., park after service there and before that in Yale, B.C., a Daly City fireman on vacation was instrumental in having the old engine returned to the city of its fame and lovingly preserved for display to future generations.

Broderick No. 1 was built in the Pine Street shop of William E. Worth, San Francisco pattern maker, in 1855. It was ordered by the Empire Engine Co. No. 1, the first volunteer company in that city. Of elegant design, using two 8½" cylinders fitted with patent air-discharging valves invented by Worth, the engine threw two streams of water and the brakes, or pumping arms, were so effective, it was claimed "near forty men can be put upon them at once." The box between the wheels holding tools and gear was built of tamanu wood imported from the South Sea islands. The hose reel fitted into a wrought iron ring, as shown in the photograph above.

In the day of hand-operated fire engines, most models were built in New York, Rhode Island, Baltimore and other eastern centers. San Francisco, true to its early habit of nonconformity, would have none of this and insisted upon building its own fire engine. In that way it would have no one to blame but itself should the apparatus not be a success.

But the engine came up to full expectations and the city was vastly proud of its achievement.

When it was rescued from obscurity, purchased by Fireman's Fund Insurance Company and brought home to San Francisco, the newspapers hailed the event with enthusiasm worthy of a prodigal son. There was a parade along California and Montgomery Streets and a formal welcome from Mayor Roger D. Lapham. The Broderick was home to stay.

SACRAMENTO ENGINE (page 99) from reverse side.

The Sacramento was famous end-stroke engine

In use by the Seattle Fire Department and other companies on the Pacific Coast, the Sacramento was an adaptation of the original end-stroke pumper developed by William C. Hunneman, an apprentice of Paul Revere and Ephriam Thayer of Massachusetts. Their engines were used extensively throughout New England and Canada.

In operation, eight to twelve men grasped the pumping arms or brakes at each side of the wheels, pushing down as the rocker arm brought up the brakes at the other end. Each up-and-down motion constituted a stroke and 60 to 80 strokes could be made every minute. At such speeds, men could last without rest at the brakes for some ten minutes; less, if they were under stress to pump faster.

(Above) SIDE-ARM pumping engine and hose cart, Virginia City, Nevada, November 1863.

WESTINGHOUSE gasoline fire engine pumped 600 gallons per minute, was powered by 40 H.P. engine, used by Seattle Fire Department.

"In the mass of flame

START OF BIG BLAZE, June 6, 1889. First Avenue looking north, smoke rolling up from under Madison Street side of Pontius Block.

"Had a professional arson ring planned to destroy Seattle on the afternoon of June 6, 1889, it would have chosen the rear of the Pontius Block as the ideal location to set the torch. Conditions were perfect — a long dry spell, the wind in the right direction, and the frame buildings lining the narrow streets were made to order for the rapid spread of a conflagration. On that afternoon the "torch" was set — quite by accident — the torch being a pot of glue in a basement cabinet shop in the rear of the Pontius Block at what is now First Avenue and Madison Street.

"Jim McGough's cabinet shop in the basement of the Pontius Block was a beehive of activity on that afternoon, with five cabinetmakers working to fill a stack of orders which had been pouring in. About 2:15 p.m., a pot of glue boiled over on the hot stove and set fire to some shavings on the floor. . . .

"One of the men at the cabinet shop, John E. Back, dashed a pail of water against the flames, washing the burning glue onto a pile of dry shavings on the floor. What happened after that is not quite clear, but apparently the men attempted to subdue the flames by forming a bucket brigade, but when the fire got away, all hands retreated in great confusion to the street. . . ."

Clarence B. Bagley in his *History of Seattle* published in 1916 presents the city of that day. "The town's rapid growth during the late '80s developed conditions ripe for the conflagration which every American city apparently has to have at some early period in its history. North of Columbia Street and on the west side of First Avenue was a row of frame structures mostly two stories in height, and with a sawmill, lumber yards and many wooden sheds between them and the wharves. Even the pavements were plank. Streets as well as buildings were generally on posts or piles, and well above the ground or water, leaving a space below through which the fire could travel without hindrance. The public water supply was at as high a pressure as is furnished now in the same

locality, but the mains were small, the hydrants of limited capacity and only at alternate streets. . . ."

The Bundy report details the fire-fighting equipment. "Between 1884 and 1889, the population had increased tremendously, (from 3,533 in 1880 to 42,837 in 1890), but the defenses had remained the same. Its two little steam pumpers were capable of supplying only three good 2½-inch streams, barely enough to control an ordinary residence fire. The water, excellent for domestic purposes, was sadly inadequate for fire streams.

"The Seattle Volunteer Fire Department at the time of the great fire was no 'comic opera' type of organization. It was a matter of great personal pride to belong to one of the hose companies. Only young men of good physique and character, who were also good athletes, were accepted. Competitive tournaments were staged annually between Seattle, Victoria, B.C., Bellingham, Port Townsend, Snohomish, Tacoma, Olympia, Portland and Spokane. Seattle was always the team to beat.

"At fires, the competition between Seattle's two engine companies was intense. Each company gave its all to beat the other company to the fire and get first water at the base of the blaze — a tradition that has carried over to the present day, as companies still consider being 'first-in' or 'stealing the fire' from another company, a matter of pride.

"Seattle's Engine #1 was a third-size Gould steam pumper, purchased in 1879 and housed in a brick engine house on Columbia Street, west of Second Avenue. Engine #2 was a fourth-size Gould steam pumper purchased in 1882 and housed in the brick combination engine house and City Hall, south of Yesler Way on Third Avenue. The famed hand engine, Sacramento, had been sent to the Western Mills, about Terry Avenue and Republican Street, in 1882 and played no part in the fire.

"Hose #7, a four-wheel reel, was in service in the old North School, Third Avenue and Pine Street, and Hose #4 was in service at First Avenue and Battery Street. The two steam pumpers had been provided horses and a paid driver in 1888. Hose #4 had one horse and a a driver. The rest of the equipment was hand-drawn by sturdy volunteers. Ladder #1, a 65'

This account is part of the study made by Lieut. George A. Bundy, Seattle Fire Department, retired, and is an authentic report on the fire defenses and fire action. The more detailed historical account is taken from "History of Seattle" by Clarence B. Bagley as noted in the text.

FIRST AVENUE looking toward Madison where fire was first noticed — street level view of same scene as one on page 104.

Preston aerial truck, purchased in 1887 for $765.00, was housed in a shed at what is now Occidental and King Street. The aerial ladder was a new invention and not yet perfected. It was considered a 'white elephant.' No horses were provided for the truck, the volunteers were forced to hire horses whenever they had to respond to a fire. In responding to alarms, the two steamers also hauled hose reels along behind.

"The fate of the City of Seattle was entrusted to a handful of dedicated volunteers, organized in May 1884, with Gardner Kellogg (later to become one of the men directly responsible for Seattle's present-day excellent department), as its first Fire Chief. In May of 1888, Josiah (Joe) Collins was elected Chief by the Board of Fire delegates. The day of the fire Collins was absent, in California. . . ."

Writes Clarence Bagley: "About 2:45 in the beautiful summer afternoon of the 6th of June 1889, (Bundy's research places the time about

2:15 and the time the alarm was received as 2:45) "a cloud of smoke rolled from under the Madison Street side of the Pontius Block, and steam whistles along the waterfront at once blew the repeated blasts that signaled the outbreak of fire. Engine house bells followed with a continuous jingle, and from the nearest fire station on Columbia Street, at the alley below Second, there came a hose-cart pulled by men and boys. Behind them a team of horses drew the town's first steam engine, but this was stopped and attached to the hydrant at Columbia. The firemen were confronted by a great mass of smoke and could scarcely determine where to throw the water but started a stream from the Madison Street hydrant on the Pontius Building. . . ."

The Bundy brief describes the action from a fireman's viewpoint.

"By the time the first engine company arrived, a huge crowd had gathered to watch the fire, many wondering why the fire department

POST-INTELLIGENCER.

VOL. XVI.   SEATTLE, WASHINGTON, FRIDAY, JUNE 7, 1889.   NO. 27.

A SEA OF FIRE

The Business Part of Seattle in ——

Sixty-Four Acres of Ground Swept.

Thirty-Two Blocks of Smoking Debris.

The Loss Will Exceed Ten Millions.

A Little Blaze at Madison Street Becomes a Giant of Destruction, Ravaging All the Lowlands to the South—Fire-Proof Brick and Frail Wood Alike Food for the Forked Tongues—The Phœnix.

"A SEA OF FIRE," headlined *Seattle Post-Intelligencer* of June 7, 1889, day following fire that gave Seattle crippling blow.

HOTEL LINCOLN at 4th and Madison burning in 1920.

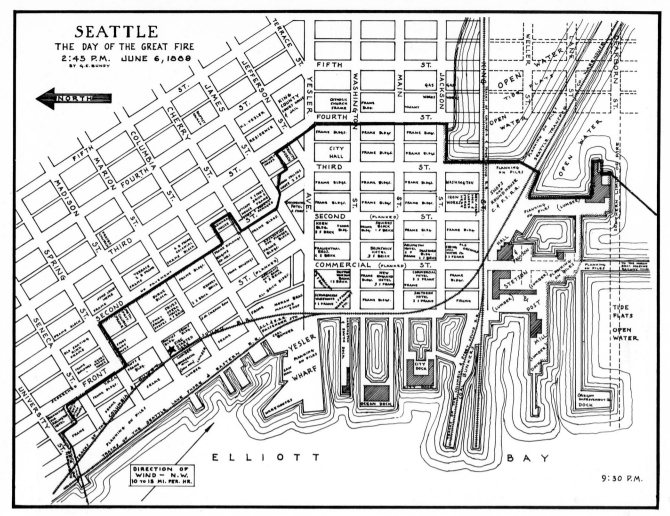

AREA COVERED by Seattle fire of 1889 — drawn by Lieut. George A. Bundy, Seattle Fire Department, retired.

didn't arrive. Apparently no one thought it necessary to call. Before the first hose line was stretched, considering the poor water supply and the inadequate fire defenses — the City of Seattle was doomed.

"Engine #1 arrived at the scene within two or three minutes after receipt of the alarm. Two hand lines were laid from the front of the building back to the closest hydrant, Front and Columbia. Engine #2, moments later, went around the north side of the building on Madison Street and took suction from Elliott Bay through planking in the street. They laid their line into the basement, to the base of the fire.

"Hose #7 laid its line from the hydrant at Front and Madison to the north side of the building, while Hose #4 took the hydrant at Spring and Front and joined the other two companies on the north side of the building.

"The response to the fire was fast, the lines well placed, and normally the blaze would have

been confined to the place of origin and quickly extinguished. Only one thing was wrong — the fire was out of control, the water supply quickly failed — and within seven hours, Seattle's business district and waterfront would be a sea of glowing embers.

"As the fire continued to progress, the heat on the north side of the building began to burn the hose. The Commercial Mill building across the alley also started to burn, forcing Engine #2 to abandon their position. They moved south one block to Marion Street and tried to take suction from Elliott Bay, but the tide was wrong. Another attempt was made from Columbia Street with the same result.

"Meanwhile, the huge Opera House across Front Street at Marion caught fire. Engine #1 attempted to get streams on this structure as well as the Pontius Block. The water pressure was failing fast. Firemen were able to gain entry into the building but the water supply by this time was so poor, there wasn't enough

COLORED LITHOGRAPH displayed and distributed by Crawford and Conover, Seattle real estate firm, after great fire of 1889.

CHARLES T. CONOVER.
Seattle.

DIAMOND & CONOVER
REAL ESTATE BROKERS

TESLER-LEARY BLOCK

OCCIDENTAL HOTEL

NOT A DISASTER

Although Seattle's great fire caused losses aggregating $15,000,000.00 to $18,-000,000.00, the business men and citizens, with cheerful faces and brave hearts, met in mass meeting the next morning and accepted the seeming calamity as a benefit rather than a disaster. Every prominent property owner stated his intention of building better and higher than before. The city council at once straightened and widened the business streets. Before the debris was cold it was being removed by an army of laborers and construction was begun on hundreds of new brick blocks. In the future, even more than in the past, Seattle will be entitled to be known as the Queen City and pride of Washington. Its people are the embodiment of indomitable pluck and energy, and investments here are more sought after now than ever before.

DEALERS IN
PROVISIONS
BADLY BENT
BUT NOT BROKEN

BUSINESS RESUMED

TACOMA RELIEF BUREAU
MEALS AND LODGINGS
FURNISHED FREE
TO THE NEEDY

At a public meeting held at Seattle the day after the fire, the question was asked—
"Shall the money collected for the Johnstown sufferers be used for the relief of sufferers at .... home?"

Hundreds of Voices:—"NO! NO! LET HER GO!"

JUNE 6, 1889. LOSS $15,000,000.

Sketched by Special Artists and Engraved especially for Crawford & Conover, by The West Shore Magazine, Portland, Oregon.

pressure to lift the water one floor into the building, and they were forced to abandon any hope of saving the structure.

"At this point the crowd was in a carnival mood, still treating the fire as a large joke. As the streams continued to become more feeble, the crowd began to jeer the volunteers. Engine #1 was forced to pick up their equipment and retreat to Columbia Street. The hydrant there was of no use. They moved to Cherry Street with no better luck. At this time the water pressure had been so reduced that a stream from the hydrants would not reach ten feet.

"After a short conference between the commanding officers, it was decided the best move was to attempt to save their equipment, and both Engine #1 and #2 retreated to Third Street and Yesler Avenue, while Hose #4 and #7 moved north to Spring Street and Front Street. Seattle's Mayor, Robert Moran, took command and ordered buildings in the path of the fire dynamited. This only provided good kindling for the unquenchable blaze which now advanced towards the Skid Road, a roaring inferno. . . ."

The Bagley history continues with a more detailed description of the fire's progress. "To the north the danger did not appear so imminent for the breeze from the bay was apparently a protection. Westward the sheds and lumber belonging to the Commercial Mill were blazing in spots and the employees were waging a futile fight with their own hose lines. On the southern side the Marion Street end of the Colman Block was smoking in the great heat: this was a two-story frame row reaching to Columbia. At this time men appeared with hose from the steamer that had then commenced to pump from salt water, but they could not get near enough to the Colman Block to wet it down: the side and roof burst into flame and the conflagration was started on its southerly course. The Opera House was then well on fire.

"Realizing that a great disaster was impending, telegrams asking for help were sent to Victoria, Portland and all the larger towns between. For two or three blocks to the east and south, people were moving stocks of goods, law libraries and all sorts of personal belongings. Over the fire rose an enormous column of rolling and twisting smoke which could be plainly seen from Tacoma, and with it a shower of sparks and brands. Some of the latter alighted on an old frame building near what is now the southeast corner of Western Avenue and Columbia, and presently a furious fire was raging there. Before the main conflagration had burned a third of the Colman row, flames from this old structure had set fire to the rear of the Union Block, which was a three-story brick building next south of the San Francisco store, at First Avenue and Columbia. At this juncture, a party of men under the able leadership of Mayor Robert Moran fired heavy charges of explosives under the Palace Restaurant in the Colman Block, but while the building was shattered, an effective gap was not made and the fire swept onward. Several other attempts were just as unsuccessful.

"There being only an excavation where the Burke Block was later built, on the northwest corner of Second and Marion, furniture and scenery from Frye's Opera House were piled there, only to be burned in the great heat from the theater. There were then only two brick buildings on the east side of First Avenue, north of James; these were the Reinig, across Marion from the Opera House, and the Kenney at the end of the same block at Columbia. The former, occupied by Harms and Dickman, was quickly in a blaze, and the wooden buildings to the east and south took fire almost as speedily. At 4 o'clock the flames were crossing Columbia west of First Avenue; five minutes later the Kenney Block was burning on the roof, and at 4:40 p.m. its walls were falling. The small frame structures along Second from the paint store of Harris and Greenus at Marion, to the hardware store of McLaughlin and Bridges at Columbia, went down one after the other, but being low the heat was not so great as to prevent, by strenuous efforts, the saving of the Colonial Block, a two-story frame row on the northeast corner of Second and Columbia. A line of shade trees here gave considerable protection. On the Haller corner it was noted that a stream from a fire hose would not reach the roof on the one-story building, so much had the water pressure diminished. This was at 4:15 p.m.

"The flames were then raging from Second to the Bay, and from Columbia nearly to Spring, for the intense heat in the vicinity of First Avenue and Madison was spreading the fire northward against the wind. In this direction the first to go were the two-story frame buildings on the northwest and northeast corners of the latter streets. The former was called the Kenyon Block and contained the

(Above) "SMALL FRAME STRUCTURES went down one after the other," wrote Clarence Bagley in his *History of Seattle*.

(Below) S L and E DEPOT from docks below the fire which raged on the streets above.

Times printing establishment; the other was owned by M. R. Maddocks and occupied by a drug store. Along the waterfront a furious fire was raging, fed by Colman's and other large wharves, the warehouses of Staver and Walker, Knapp Burrell and Company and others, and the great Commercial Mill with all its lumber; the bucket brigades and firemen were driven back again and again. On the southeast corner of First Avenue and Spring, the excavation for the Holyoke Block gave a chance, and finding that the fire was not likely to cross Spring on that side, a determined and successful fight was made to save the Amos Brown house, on the northeast corner of First Avenue and that street. It was a strategic point, for in the rear of this frame building was a very large wooden structure, once used as a skating rink, and directly opposite it on Second, a frame church. The fire would have gone from one to the other across Second, and then up the hill into the residence district. Luckily the Brown residence stood, but the scorched paint and broken glass showed what an effort was made. The same struggle was continued up First Avenue and the fire did not get across above Spring. It swept north, however, in spite of determined opposition, with the inadequate means at hand, destroying among other large buildings, the Northwestern Cracker Company's factory and the plant of the Seattle Electric Light Company and the Seattle Ice concern. Fortunately, on the southwest corner of University was the open area formed by the foundation of what was later the Arlington Hotel, and west of that a clear space crossed only by the railroad trestles, and there the fire was brought to a halt. It was 8:30, though, before this was certain.

"Columbia Street was no obstacle to the onward sweep of the conflagration toward the south. An effort to blow up the White Building on the southeast corner of First Avenue was a failure. The firemen and a host of willing volunteers were helpless. The line of fire crossed, with the portion west of First Avenue considerably in advance; it seized upon the fire station back of the present Hinckley Block and soon the bell fell from the tower with a great crash. When it involved Boyd's photograph gallery, on the southwest corner of Second, the window casings of the large brick Boston Block commenced to smoke and the glass cracked. Nearly everyone thought the building doomed, but by heroic efforts with pails, pans and anything that would hold water, the

(Opposite) PUGET SOUND NATIONAL BANK after 1889 fire. (Above) Pioneer Place, June 7.

(Below) RUINS OF YESLER SAWMILL after 1889 fire destroyed most of Seattle business property.

(Above) DEVASTATED AREA from Second and Cherry looking toward Elliott Bay. (Below) Three views of Seattle ruins after 1889 fire.

windows were protected until the greatest heat of the fire had passed by. The post office, then in this building, was partly moved, but was in order again by night. No other brick building was left unburned in the business district. Some small frame structures in the same block south of it were destroyed.

"Meanwhile the fire progressed down First Avenue, through the solid row of brick buildings on the west side of the street from Columbia to Yesler. The San Francisco Store, (Toklas-Singerman's), the Union Block, the Poncin, Starr, Arcade and Yesler-Leary, were one after the other in flames, the last about 6 o'clock. This was the most imposing array of buildings Seattle had. Back of them to the bay everything was on fire, down to Moran's machine shop on Yesler. On the east side of the street, the frame stores burned steadily, the fire reaching Cherry at 5 p.m. On Second the St. Charles Hotel, on the northwest corner of Cherry, blazed with an intense heat, but in spite of this the Wyckoff House on the southeast corner was saved. This stood where the Alaska Building now is. Not far from 5 o'clock the wind changed about and blew from a more southerly direction, giving new spirit to the fire fighters, but it soon changed back again to the regular northwestern summer breeze. The Tacoma firemen came in about that time, having made the run over the Northern Pacific in sixty-three minutes. Unfortunately, there was no engine in Tacoma at the date, so they brought only a hose carriage and hose which were of little use after the water pressure failed. However, they worked very hard, and so did another detail from the same city, which arrived at 7:50 p.m. with more hose.

"At 6:30 the fire reached the Occidental Hotel at James, Second and Yesler. This was the town's most pretentious hotel and many thought it fireproof. The Pioneer Block corner at First Avenue and James was then an open excavation but a three-story frame building on the Butler property at the corner of Second burned fiercely and warmed up the Occidental until clouds of smoke came from each of its four stories. All at once it burst into flame with a roar like an explosion and filled Yesler Avenue with fire; the heat was so tremendous that people nearby had to run for their lives. Buildings on the south side of Yesler took fire instantly, and even the Collins house, across Second, was in a blaze so rapidly that its inmates could barely escape. From the Collins place the fire extended up the hill to Trinity Church, and the prisoners were hastily removed from the courthouse at Third and Yesler to save their lives. But the fire did not cross that street and swept to the southerly limit along its western side. In the b l o c k below Yesler there was quite a fight to save Father Prefontaine's church when the fire went by across the street, and happily this was a success.

"When the fire crossed Yesler it simply ran riot among the frame buildings on the 'flats.' From Third South to the bay it moved with a whirlwind of its own making in front. There was no time to save goods and not very much to save life; by 9:30 it had carried devastation as far as there was anything to burn and then stopped for lack of material.

(Above, left) FIRST AND CHERRY after the big fire. (Center) Remains of Occidental Hotel at James, Second and Yesler. (Right) Front Street ruins.

"The night of June 6th is a memorable time in the annals of Seattle. Most of the city was brightly illuminated by the flames which still covered 116 acres of what had been the most valuable part of the town. In the red glare men gathered in groups discussing the disaster which had befallen them and making plans for the future. They could see that destruction was complete in practically the entire business district. Nothing but broken walls remained of the city's mercantile row; the continuous line of brick buildings from Columbia to Yesler on the west side of First Avenue including the stores of Toklas and Singerman, Chillberg & Co., Griffith Davies, the Bank of Commerce, R. L. Durant, Charles Goldstein, L. A. Treen, Herschberg & Co., Baillargeon & Co., the Merchants National Bank, the Gordon Hardware, Stewart and Holmes, the Seattle Hardware Co., W. P. Boyd, Pumphrey & Co., and Albert Hanson. West of First Avenue and south of University Street, for a distance of four-fifths of a mile, every wharf, warehouse, mill, factory, machine shop and lumber yard was utterly destroyed, and the waterfront was nothing but blazing timbers and piles. The east side of First Avenue and west side of Second were in ruins from the southern tide flats to Spring Street on the north; on the eastern side of Second all was gone below the Boston Block except some small buildings between Cherry and James, and this destruction extended east to what are now Third Avenue South and Third Avenue as far north as James.

"The district below Yesler had been the business center up to a year or two before; at the time of the fire it contained mostly frame hotels and lodging houses of the most combustible character. Schwabacher's large wholesale house was on Yesler just west of First Avenue South, and Gardner Kellogg's drug store next to it. Mr. Kellogg, like many another volunteer fireman, lost the chance to save his goods by fighting the fire. The Washington Iron Works had a large plant on Jackson Street and Second Avenue South. There were also many extensive warehouses and wharves, notably those of the Pacific Coast Company. At the latter were the steamships *Mexico* and *Ancon*, which loaded their decks with personal belongings brought to them for safekeeping and then drew out into the bay. This was likewise done by smaller craft at other points.

"The calls upon other cities for assistance brought the Tacoma contingents promptly, as has been stated. Some firemen came from other localities, but without apparatus. The next to arrive were a party of volunteers from Olympia just before midnight; these brought a Silsby steam fire engine in less than four hours on the little steamer *Fleetwood*. Some time later a train from Portland drew in with another Silsby engine and firemen from that city, but were much delayed in finding a place to

118

unload. At 4 o'clock the steamer *T. J. Potter* arrived with more volunteers and an English Merriwether engine from Victoria; they left home at 11 and could see the glow of the conflagration in the sky from the very start. No other engines came, because there were no more in the state, except at great distances away. All these firemen went to work with a will and made themselves extremely useful during the rest of the night and the next day. Most of the time their machines were worked from vessels or barges in the bay.

"In the late afternoon calls were sent out to all members of the militia companies to report at the armory forthwith, and the soldier boys responded so promptly as to be there to take charge of the county prisoners brought up from the jail about 7 o'clock. In order to attract attention to the call, Col. J. C. Haines, of the First Regiment, N.G.W., mounted his horse in full uniform and rode about the streets just outside the fire district. After it was seen that the courthouse would not burn, the soldiers escorted the prisoners back to Third and Yesler again. The other companies of the regiment were called out and arrived during the next day; the downtown portion of the city was kept under martial law for about two weeks, with headquarters at the armory on Union Street between Third and Fourth.

"Mayor Robert Moran called a public meeting in the evening at the courthouse and 200 special deputies were s w o r n in to preserve order. Relief measures were inaugurated at once and telegrams offering assistance came in that night. In Tacoma the citizens went to work at once preparing food and supplies, and at dawn sent over a boatload of provisions. The weather was fortunately fine and there was no such distress as there would have been had the fire gone up the hill into the residence district. Great tents for the homeless were set up the next day, and the ladies' relief organizations saw to it that no one went hungry.

"The published list of losses footed up an adding machine total of $7,179,725 and adding $1,100,000, which is an estimated figure for the losses of the City of Seattle in streets, docks, etc., makes $8,279,725. There is no mention in the lists of the Water Company or the Electric Light Co. for their losses on their mains, wires and poles in the burned district. The figure for the City of Seattle may be high. On the strength of the value of personal effects in lodge houses and hotels, added to the foregoing figures, the total loss has been placed as high as $20,000,000, but this is out of all reason. . . .

"The dawn of June 7 marks the birth of a new Seattle. With the first light, the ruin-lined streets were full of animation. The city did not give itself time to cool off. Its people were ready and anxious for the task of reconstruction. The *Post-Intelligencer* upheld its newspaper supremacy by appearing a few minutes after 4 a.m., though its entire plant had been wiped out of existence just twelve hours before. It was followed a little later by the *Morning Journal*. . . .

BURNED-OUT SEATTLE AREA, looking southwest toward Elliott Bay from Second and Cherry.

"Seven hours later, at 11 o'clock, the people of the stricken city met in Armory Hall to plan for immediate reconstruction. Mayor Robert Moran presided and about him were seated 600 citizens, each one an active businessman. No one would have imagined these men were in the midst of a calamity. It was a meeting representative of the city's best energy, hope and confidence. By unanimous vote it was resolved to prohibit forever the erection of any wooden structures in the burned district. After telegrams offering assistance had been read, a relief committee was appointed to take charge of all money, clothing and provisions received for distribution. Permits were granted for the erection of tents for the temporary transaction of business in the burned district.

"Just as in every other crisis which Seattle has faced in its history, the city brought forth its strong fighting men. Previous to the fire several thousand dollars had been raised for the sufferers of the Johnstown flood, but the money had not been sent when the fire broke out. A suggestion made at the meeting that the money raised for Johnstown should be diverted for the urgent need at home was promptly howled down, the whole meeting, with one great voice, shouting 'Send the money to Johnstown!'

"In a stirring speech, Judge Cornelius Hanford scorned the suggestion that Seattle should take the money that was already pledged to the eastern sufferers. Judge John P. Hoyt, then a power in the financial world, pledged the support of the banks to the efforts of the people to rebuild on the ruins. Angus Mackintosh and Jacob Furth promised that their respective banks would be of all the assistance possible and would not make any effort to profit by the fire. Watson C. Squire struck the chord that was dominant in the meeting when he stated that he was ready to commence building and was merely waiting until the bricks of the old structure became cool enough to remove.

"One of the brightest spots in the story of Seattle's fortunate misfortune was the immediate offers of aid, especially from Tacoma. As soon as news of the fire was known, cities and towns throughout the Northwest vied with one another in aiding Seattle, though no appeal for aid had been made. Tacoma was the first city to respond. On the night of June 6th, Allen C. Mason employed all the bakers in that city at his own expense, and at dawn the next morning dispatched a boatload of provisions to Seattle. The same morning the Tacoma Relief Bureau established headquarters on the present site of the Federal Building at Third and Union. Samuel Collier, cashier of the Merchants National Bank, was placed in charge of the subscription list. Large tents for feeding and housing the homeless were supplied. In addition to this, Tacoma in one hour raised $10,000 cash for relief and subsequently made its cash contribution double that amount. San Francisco sent $10,000 cash; Olympia $1,000; Virginia City, Nevada, $4,000, and other towns accordingly.

"On the 12th, 200 men were set to work with teams to clear the streets of debris in the burned district. All workmen were given employment at once at good wages to build up 'New Seattle.'

"The sales of real estate were checked only for a few days and regained their activity by the time agents and owners could find places to carry on business; meanwhile outside capital poured in from all over the country for investment. The reconstruction of electric and cable lines of the street railways, totally destroyed in the burned district, was begun almost immediately.

"For the first twenty days after the fire more than forty-one thousand meals were served in the Tacoma relief tent. 'Tacoma's extraordinary relief work did a great deal to heal the breach that existed between the two cities,' says Welford Beaton in *The City That Made Itself*, 'and no matter what the future may bring forth for these two leading cities on Puget Sound, Seattle should never forget that in the hour of her direst need Tacoma stood nobly by her, fed her people and gave as bountifully of her money as her food.'

"The women of Seattle also aided in the relief work, converting Armory Hall into a vast dining room. Within a month the general relief committee of Seattle, composed of J. R. Lewis, E. P. Ferry, John Leary, Griffith Davies and George H. Heilbron had received total cash contributions of $98,805.

"The resumption of business was immediate. A few business blocks and houses on the east side of Second Avenue remained undestroyed and these became the headquarters of industry. The office of Moore Land Company on the corner of Second and James was the nucleus of the new business center. For twelve blocks on either side Second Avenue became a lane of tents and projected buildings.

"For many days the banking and commer-

RIALTO BUILDING, Seattle, Washington, on fire May 24, 1929, photographed from Second and Madison.

HENRY YESLER MANSION looms up on hillside overlooking tents and rubble of June 1889 fire.

cial business of the city was transacted under canvas roofs. Thirty days after the fire eighty-eight brick buildings to cost more than three million dollars were either under way or projected for transformed Seattle.

"A splendid spirit of courage and faith took possession of every heart; adversity made friends. As soon as the cooling of the embers would permit, tents and temporary structures made their appearance all over the burned district. The public schools, which had closed temporarily, were reopened on Monday, June 10th. Large quantities of lost goods were gathered up by orders of the mayor and returned to owners as far as they could be ascertained. Contributions from all parts of the United States soon began to arrive. Every business firm in the city received telegrams from their eastern supply houses offering to send at once any quantity of goods wanted.

"The work of clearing away the wreckage was prodigious, alone costing many scores of thousands of dollars. At the beginning of the restoration serious embarrassment was experienced because there were neither railway depots nor docks for the landing of building materials. It was fully six weeks before arrangements were perfected to receive brick, iron, lumber and other materials in any considerable quantities.

The rapidity with which the city rebuilt itself sent Seattle's fame over the country. Nothing like it had been witnessed on the American continent with the single exception

of Chicago during the period immediately succeeding the great fire of 1871. Within a year there was accomplished inside the limits of the burned district a general building construction nearly matching the total loss of buildings and merchandise in the fire. . . ."

Writing again of the fire department activity, George Bundy states: "After the fire, the fire department rented a barn on University Street, just east of Third Avenue, to house its equipment. The citizens, refusing to accept the blame for the fire, began to criticize the volunteers. A succession of chiefs followed: On July 10, Josiah Collins resigned; on August 2, Jack McDonald was appointed, in September, he resigned.

"Seattle did not inaugurate a paid fire department because it wanted to — it was forced to take this step. The volunteer companies disbanded in disgust and only a few were willing to ever serve again. On October 21, Gardner Kellogg was persuaded to take over the position of rebuilding the Seattle Fire Department and was appointed the first paid Fire Chief.

"Chief Kellogg took a firm hand in dealing with the disgruntled citizens who were still critical of the fire department. He issued a public statement, 'Had the best fire department in the world been on the scene at the time, the results would have been the same.' In rebuilding, Kellogg was able to attract some outstanding firefighters to Seattle, recruiting from Chicago, St. Paul, and other eastern cities."

(Above, left) MILITIA AND CITIZENS at information tent in yard of Denny home at 3rd and Union. (Center) Tent stores of Rosenfeld, Smith Co. and Chester Cleary. (Right) Inside tent store at 2nd and Cherry.

(Left) HOMELESS, JOBLESS, FOODLESS victims of 1889 Seattle fire get emergency help at tent set up by Tacoma Relief Bureau.

(Above) GRAND TRUNK DOCK burning July 30, 1914; fireboat *Duwamish* at right.

(Below) BILLOWS OF BLACK SMOKE and water spray make pattern as fireboat *Duwamish* fights Montana Lumber Yard fire.

FIREMAN WRESTLES with heavy nozzle as fire boat *Duwamish* works in close to burning Grand Trunk Dock, 1914.

Spokane . . . 1889—"A night of terror, devastation and awful woe . . . !"

"Sunday, August 4, 1889, became memorable as the date of the 'great fire.' The flames originated in a row of frame buildings near the corner of Railroad Avenue and Post Street, just opposite the old Northern Pacific passenger station. There had been no rain for many weeks and fierce forest fires were burning in the Coeur d'Alenes. A dense cloud of smoke hung over the city, sometimes obscuring the sun. On the first anniversary of the conflagration the *Review* retold the story of that fiery evening:

"The blaze seemed a trifling affair and a bystander watching it before the firemen arrived remarked: 'Six men could check the fire with buckets, the firemen will have it under control in a few minutes.' The fire department arrived promptly and worked well, but there was no water. Men ran from one hydrant to another, while others impatiently held the nozzles of the empty hose.

"The flames increased, slowly burning their way from the roof of the two-story building to the lower story and gradually extended to the adjacent houses which almost filled the entire block.

"Darkness came on and the assembled crowd moved back in amazement as the flames mounted higher to the sky. Mayor Furth galloped into the crowd on horseback, then galloped away to look after the water supply. The situation became alarming and whisperings were heard that the city was doomed. Word went round that Superintendent Jones, of the water works was out of town and the

This account is taken from "History of the City of Spokane" by N. W. Durham, 1912.

"APPALLING CALAMITY visits proud city of Spokane Falls"—August 4, 1889.

man in charge of the pumping station was unacquainted with the machinery. The whole block of frame buildings was ablaze and the flames had created a high wind. The Pacific Hotel stood near, then one of the handsomest structures in the city. Before water came, its front began to yield, the plate glass began to crackle, curling clouds of smoke crept through the openings and arrows of flame shot through the swirling smoke banks.

"Then came the panic, for the people realized that no power could check the conflagration. Hundreds hurried away to save their own effects. Every available vehicle was brought into requisition and fabulous sums were offered for assistance in the salvage of valuables. In less time than it takes to relate the story, the dome of the Pacific fell with a crash and a whirlwind arose that speedily swept over the block adjoining northward. In a moment that block was ablaze.

"The scene was both grand and appalling, but there was work to be done. Those who

had gone to the telegraph office to inform that a fire was raging here, went again and found that building in flames. Shrieks of women and children commingled with the commanding tones of the teamsters, the firemen and thousands of other voices, all of which were drowned by the roar of the sea of fire.

"People supposed at first that such buildings as the Hyde block, Eagle, Tull, Granite and the Frankfurt would prove a barrier, but even these went down like children's playhouses. On the destroyer swept until the river was reached. All the banks, all the hotels, the postoffice, the land office, all the large business houses were destroyed in less than four hours from the time the alarm sounded. Every pound of giant powder that could be obtained was used in the blowing up of buildings on corners and by this means much valuable property was saved.

"At the river masses of burning shingles and even flaming timbers floated northward in the air, igniting the mills on the other side, but by great effort and the judicious use of the little dynamite that was left, the fire was conquered there. Several bridges were destroyed but the Washington and Post Street crossings were saved. Over these a terrified and motley stream af homeless people passed, seeking shelter under the pine trees and relief from the smoke and heat and din of the ruins. They were not heavily burdened, for there were few downtown dwellers who had time to save anything of value. Some had blankets, others pillows and a few carried bundles on their backs, but most of them were scantily attired and bankrupt of all personal effects. Among the latter were many theatrical and 'sporting' people, who were in great distress, for they lost not only all they possessed, but their means of earning a livelihood was gone.

"Before the midnight train on the Northern Pacific was due, a rush was made for the depot. A scene of turmoil and destruction was there presented. The tracks had been destroyed all the way from Monroe to Washington Street; the telegraph wires and poles were down for a greater distance. Men and women from the telegraph office were at work, tapping the wires at both sides of the burned district to accommodate the thousands who were clamoring for means of communication with the outer world. The clanging of the church bells had ceased, but still there were shriekings of locomotives and hoarse shouts of men in the

(Above) SOUTHWEST CORNER Lincoln and Riverside from Commercial Hotel after fire.
Legend on photo incorrect.

railroad yards, seeking to save the company's effects. Both passenger and freight depots were gone and blazing cars were hauled away to protect the long trains that stood on the side tracks.

"Thirty-two blocks in the heart of the city had been destroyed. No vestige of their former grandeur remaining, save the blackened walls and smoldering wrecks in basements.

"The conflagration was under control by nine o'clock and before midnight the city was placed under military laws. Ropes were stretched across the principal streets and lines were plainly marked. Notices were issued forbidding intrusion upon the stricken territory. Badges were issued those who could show that business demanded their admittance, but others were strictly refused, for the city was filled with thieves.

"Great alarm was felt lest there might be much suffering for want of provisions and appeals for aid went out over the wires. Subsequent facts afterwards demonstrated that this alarm was unfounded, for a few carloads

of supplies, for which most of the people in need of them were amply able to pay, would have been sufficient, but the panic was so great that the officials were possibly justified in their calls for assistance and the response came promptly, bountifully and overwhelmingly. Money was not needed, yet thousands of dollars came by wire, mail and by express. Tents came from Fort Sherman and Walla Walla and blankets, quilts and clothing from other sources sufficient to supply an army. Bacon was corded up like wood in a forest and hams were shipped in by the ton with whole carloads of canned goods. Pickles, preserves and other delicacies accumulated to such an extent that a large force of men were employed to receive them.

"The actual loss in dollars and cents was never ascertained, owing to the great number of small dealers, mechanics, lodgers and others, who had lost all and carried no insurance and made no report. Thirty representatives of insurance companies were sent to adjust the losses. They found over $6,000,000. Two deaths occurred during the fire and several persons were injured. Fortunately only the business district was burned and all the residences, the schools and the churches escaped.

"When the sun came up the morning after a dismal scene was presented. Towering amid the smoke and above the glowing embers were the charred remains of stately structures. Thousands were scurrying hither and thither viewing the appalling scene. Exclamations were uttered that Spokane Falls had received its death blow. A dense smoke hung over the city and the sun wore an angry look. Despair was depicted upon many a face until a rallying voice, seemingly borne upon the breezes, swept over the throng. The effect was electrical. 'It was a blessing in disguise,' the people said, 'and the city will rise again, stronger and better than ever before.'

"The mayor and president of the board of trade called a meeting of citizens and the council jointly, and Superintendent Jones, of the water works, was permitted to resign. Committees were appointed to look after individual cases of distress. The fire limits were extended and assurance given that better protection would be afforded in the future. Additional fire apparatus was ordered by telegraph, authority was given to buy horses to draw the hose carts, an electric fire alarm was ordered. This reassured the men who had lost their fine structures and they began bidding against each other for choice locations. Before the day was ended three banks had purchased corners at Riverside and Howard at $1,000 per front foot and architects and builders were at work. Tents were erected for temporary use and all through the fall and winter thousands of men and teams were employed. The ruined walls were knocked down with dynamite and the rubbish cleared away. As soon as plans could be drawn and material obtained, grander structures were in process of construction. . . ."

G. W. Roche, who conducted a real estate business in the Frankfort block which was destroyed by the flames, related his experiences: "The scene to those who witnessed the terrible conflagration will long be remembered. The hoarse shouts of the men running in all directions, the shrieks of women and children, the rattle of the wagons, the tolling of church bells, the shrill whistles of locomotives as they hurried to and fro trying to save the cars lined on the N. P. tracks, the angry roar of the flames, the embers and shingles flying through the air, the explosion of giant powder (used in blowing up corner buildings in an effort to check the flames), all combined to make the night hideous in the extreme. . . .

"All was chaos. People rushed excitedly here and there in an endeavor to save some of their valuables. Goods were removed from the blocks only to be licked up by the flames in the streets. Fabulous prices were paid for vehicles, ranging from $50 to $500, to use in removing the more costly stocks, and often the poor distracted merchant upon carrying out his goods arrived on the sidewalk only to find his conveyance gone, the owner having accepted a better price from another.

"The Northern Pacific Railway's passenger and freight depots were burned to the ground and the tracks destroyed from Monroe to Washington Street. Yet the loyal railroad men, after Herculean efforts, succeeded in removing to places of safety a large number of cars.

"A large number of the people took refuge on the south side of the railroad, while a motley crowd interspersed liberally with an element of the sporting fraternity, fled across the Post Street bridge and there under the shelter of the pine trees, surrounded with bedding, bundles of clothing, trunks and other belongings watched the weird sight of the burning city. . . .

"I watched the start of the fire from Harry Flood's restaurant, situated on the northeast corner of First and Post Street, diagonally across from where the fire started. From the two-story lodging house the fire soon spread to the lower buildings in the block, jumped across Post to the Pacific Hotel, a magnificent structure of brick and granite.

"I saw a team hitched to a string of twelve new vehicles trying to escape the fire, but unluckily instead of continuing east on Sprague they turned up Howard Street in an endeavor to cross the tracks and were trapped and all but the team of horses were reduced to ashes. I returned to my offices in the Frankfurt block and helped in trying to save this, the best constructed four-story building in the northwest. Harry and Louis Baer and myself worked shoulder to shoulder pouring streams of water on the window frames, holding our water soaked hats before our faces in one hand and the hose in the other. But our work was futile, the heat was so terrific it crumpled the steel shutters up like tissue paper and the brick walls seemed to melt like wax. . . ."

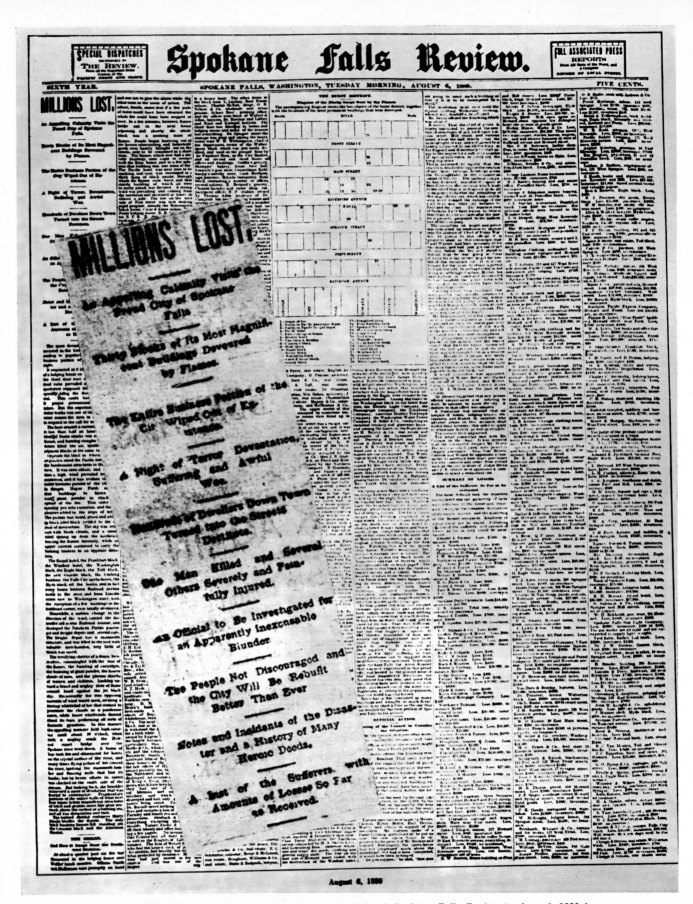

"ENTIRE BUSINESS PORTION of city wiped out," declared *Spokane Falls Review* in Aug. 6, 1889 issue.

(Above) SPOKANE FALLS' Riverside Avenue, looking east.

(Left) ARLINGTON HOTEL ruins at Howard and Main Streets.

(Right) FIRST NATIONAL BANK was only crumpled brick walls after Spokane Falls fire of Aug. 4, 1889.

(Right) TENT CITY springs up in burned area which covered 33 blocks. View of First Street looking east from Lincoln. Below is same view slightly to north.

(Opposite, center) NORTHERN PACIFIC land and Ticket Office after 1889 fire.

(Bottom, left) S P O K A N E CHRONICLE tent. (Center) Riverside from Post and Lincoln. (Right) Phoenix Stamp and Stencil Works and R. Schact, Jeweler—both in after-fire tent.

SPOKANE FALLS REVIEW, TUESDAY MORNING, AUGUST 6, 1889.

TO THE BEDLESS PUBLIC

Our Warehouses, with contents are gone. We have

WOOL MATTRESSES

Which we will sell you at

AT WHOLESALE PRICES

Have telegraphed for

SPRINGS, COTS AND BEDSTEADS.

On arrival will sell the same also at wholesale prices.

THE SPOKANE FURNITURE CO

(Above) INSURANCE AD-JUSTORS give temporary quarters air of political convention.

(Left) Beds, beds, who's got beds?

(Opposite, top and bottom) DRINK EMPORIUMS and wire services were among burned out businesses which ruined some and stimulated others.

Aberdeen . . . 1903
Scotty Campbell screamed for help

"In one blazing day, October 16, 1903, Aberdeen came of age. The big fire wiped out the city of planked streets and wooden buildings and allowed a modern kind of city to grow, one properly zoned, with better fire protection, a more substantial city with new goals and new possibilities.

"It was a Friday morning. Up country the corn was in the cribs and the harvest had been brought in from the fields. On the lower harbor the autumn mists hung low over the salt marshes and flocks of ducks rose up at the approach of a riverboat. There was the wood smoke smell from mill burners and cook stoves hanging close to the ground until midday.

This account taken from "Hometown Scrapbook," No. 39 in a series compiled by Ben Weatherwax, broadcast in 1950 by Station KBKW, Aberdeen, Washington.

"Early that morning Axel Gylfe, the photographer, was hurrying down to his studio at 60 Heron Street to develop some plates he exposed at a wedding the night before. At the Aberdeen Livery and Transfer Co. at F and Hume Streets the barn man was hitching up a team to move a load of furniture and Emil Pfund, the jeweler, was polishing his silver. Most of the sawmills were in operation and up from the busy waterfront came the whine of the saws. Jim Bowes, proprietor of the Fashion Saloon, stood in front of it at 8 Heron Street to feel the early sun and chat with Les Maley, the cigar maker and bartender Nick Larkin of Walker's Resort for Gentlemen.

"Toward 9 a.m. over in the Arctic Hotel in the Mack Building at 13 Hume Street some of the late risers were cooking breakfast on an oilstove in one of the batching rooms.

IN NINE SCORCHING HOURS 140 buildings were destroyed in Aberdeen's worst fire, Oct. 16, 1903.

SMOKE FILLS THE AIR and household goods the vacant lots as Aberdeen steadies under shock of fire.

Charles Rolfe, one of the cooks, hobbled about on his pegleg, making trips from the stove to the table.

"Suddenly there was a scream from Rolfe's room and when the others hurried there they saw it was in flames, the searing tongues licking up the thin layers of greasy wall paper and reaching for the ceiling and spreading to all parts of the old hotel. There was little time to aid Rolfe. They tried to save themselves.

"It was just 9 by the clock in the old Central School that stood about where the A. W. Barkley store is now and the school bell was calling children to classes. Suddenly above its hollow clang came the dull booming call of the city's fire bell. Members of the volunteer fire department listened. The bell was ringing wildly.

"Someone remarked that it would be a good day to test the pumper the city had just bought. As merchants and early shoppers scanned the sky for a sign of smoke, they spotted the black column beginning to rise from the corner of Hume and G Streets across from what is now the Whicher Machinery Exchange. And although the fire station was located almost next door it was several minutes before the firemen could assemble and get their equipment out. Those several minutes were critical.

"Scotty Campbell, hanging by his fingertips from the window ledge of his room in the Arctic Hotel, screamed for help. The long tongues of flame were shooting out of the windows and the fire was spreading to the roof. Chief Koehler of the Aberdeen Fire Department, took in the situation. He felt the new pumper could do the most good if it could pump out of the Wishkah River and he ordered the engine drawn to a spot not far from the west approach to the Heron Street bridge. The Department's head pumper, 'Old Tiger,' was rushed out and put into service. But by this time the Mack Building was a solid tower of flames, the fire going in three directions.

"It was moving north toward the city jail, with the roof of that building already smoking. It was threatening to jump G Street and start on the next block west and it was already burning in buildings east of the hotel. It was time for decisions and Chief Koehler made them. 'Call Cosmopolis for help,' he relayed to the telephone office. And he asked for another call to Hoquiam.

"The city jail was soon a mass of flames and police Chief Anstie turned both prisoners loose with instructions to aid in fighting the fire. By this time every member of the local fire department was on duty — Hose Company No. 1; Hook and Ladder Company No. 1; Chemical Company No. 1 and Engine Company No. 1 from the headquarters building. And as they fought the fire that building itself was going up in flames. Other hose companies were called in. No. 2 from the East side rushed across the Heron Street bridge in a body; No. 3 from over on the corner of Market and D

Streets responded and No. 4 came from the West End, their hall at Hume and Michigan.

"Before 9:30 the fire had jumped the alley and was licking at the backs of buildings facing Heron Street and merchants were frantically trying to remove their stocks ahead of the racing flames. Shopkeepers from farther west on Heron Street closed their shops to aid, and as word of the disaster spread, several mills — the West and Slade mill on the Wishkah River; the American mill farther up, and the Anderson and Middleton mill, all shut down to permit their crews to go to the assistance of the fire fighters.

"But still the fire roared. It jumped G Street into the block that included Toklas and Kaufman's brick department store building. Surely, the citizens thought, that building will withstand the flames. The fire will be stopped when it gets to that corner. But there was no stopping it. Fanned by a light morning breeze, it jumped Heron into the block between G and H Streets and began to devour one building after another. If the town is to be saved, it is now, the volunteers told each other. The fire must be stopped short of the new Elks Temple building, the George Wolff Store.

"But the area of flaming city was now so great that even with hundreds fighting the blaze, it could hardly be slowed up. It swept through the block to H Street, racing with the fire on the south side which consumed the Toklas-Kaufman brick block as though it were matchwood. At H it again leaped the street, and while it set off buildings along Heron Street, the new Fireman's Hall on the corner of Hume and H Streets seemed safe. But by now it was evident the Elks building would go. George Wolff was carrying his merchandise into the street in front of the store and stacking it in piles.

"Into the raging inferno, the volunteer fire departments of Hoquiam, Montesano and Cosmopolis arrived. The *Harbor Queen* arrived from the county seat with the firefighters, while the Hoquiam department wheeled up after a mad dash over the plank road that connected the two cities.

"It was apparent that water was no solution. Chief Koehler called a hurried conference. Something must be done quickly. It would probably have to be dynamite — then dynamite it would be. Explosive charges were placed in a building where the old Weir Theater once stood, and the roar of the explosion added to the confusion. There were also the cries of mothers looking for their children, fire fighters shouting to direct the battle against the flames. Rumors were spreading of prominent citizens who had been trapped and lost in the fire.

"With his jail empty, Chief Anstie hurriedly rounded up a troop of deputies and swore them in. The piles of merchandise stacked in the streets, the mounds of personal possessions, must be protected from looters. Soup kitchens were set up at noon or as soon as they could be organized. At the Commercial Bakery, manager Bill Murphy fed 200 homeless persons while the ladies of the W.C.T.U. ladled soup to a bread line of fire fighters and burned-out refugees.

"Seagulls swooped and screamed through the smoke and rats, burned out of their homes, scurried through the streets and under piles of goods. The new Crescent Hotel went when the fire jumped I Street, more homes were devoured and clear over to the corner of Wishkah and Broadway, the fire ate its hungry way. By six o'clock that evening it had been controlled but what had been Aberdeen was now a blackened, charred, almost unrecognizable jumble of destruction and human misery.

"The Aberdeen *Bulletin* was on the streets by nightfall with a special edition, the paper attempting to survey the loss but it was too soon. Few people slept in Aberdeen that night and by daylight souvenir hunters were scavangering through the debris. Bicyclists from Hoquiam and Cosmopolis rode over to see the awesome sight and there were plenty of citizens to provide them with a guided tour of the destruction.

"Meanwhile the townsfolk totaled up the loss. In nine scorching hours 140 buildings had been destroyed. R. T. Dabney was the heaviest loser — 18 of his 19 buildings consumed by the flames. Four lives had been lost, three of them in the old Arctic Hotel. Nearly a dozen were injured. Savings and the work of lifetimes had been blotted out in what the citizens called Black Friday.

"Less than a third had been covered by insurance. But from Seattle and Tacoma came offers of aid to the stricken city. The council met and Mayor West thanked the big towns — Aberdeen can take care of its own, was his answer, and the council dove into the heated discussion of the new fire ordinance that would provide for a permanent and substantial business district.

MEN IN HARNESS. Star Hook and Ladder team on 4th of July, Georgetown, Colorado.

Fighting Fires . . . and Each Other

It wasn't true, the *North Fork News-Nugget* said, that the fire companies brought in toughs from other towns to run those hose cart races and win them by threats, tricks and brutal means. Win them the North Fork boys did, but not with foreign talent. North Fork firemen were tough enough to beat any other team using nothing more than strong legs and arms, well — and maybe a little strong language in their boyish enthusiasm.

If the newspaper was right, North Fork was an unusual town, with unusual volunteer firemen who had unusual pride, endurance and an unusual desire to win the prize money and keep the glory of the North Fork Fire Department high. The chances were better than even the town boosters had four or six men on the racing team who were spirited into town in the small hours of the night from farms, docks or prize ring because they could outpull a Black Angus steer or pack a blacksmith's anvil under one arm.

Volunteer firemen wanted, first of all, to put out fires and be heroes at it. But there was a lot of time between fires and people could forget heroes if they weren't reminded of them. So there were parades and benefit hoe-downs and when one fire company said its hook and ladder boys could outrun those long-eared so-and-sos from up the gulch, they could keep on being heroes if they proved it.

Most regular firemen were hardy enough specimens. It took a lot of strength and backbone to pull a ton or two of cranky fire engine over a mile of dirt. No lightweight who never lifted anything heavier than a pair of kings in a stud game could last at the pumping brakes longer than it took the marshal to collar the Chinaman who started the fire. If a fellow couldn't rattle up a thirty-foot ladder through choking smoke and put his head through a pane of hot glass, he'd better stay in the store and sell suspenders.

But then a team had to beat another team and to be pretty sure it did, it had to smuggle in extras from up country. No harm in it. Give the strong boys a few square meals and some silver dollars and maybe they would stay in town and be on the force regularly. "So grab the tow rope, Charlie, and let's be first whether it's getting to the fire before South Fork does or running that 400 feet to the hotel cistern like Kelly-in-front-of-the-devil and beating the stuffings out of that bunch of glue-feet."

Get there first. In the pioneer days of the West there were no race horses, no professional baseball games, no state fair prizes, no organized sport competition of any kind. People were contest-starved and hungry to beat somebody, to fight-fight-fight, to get there first, wherever it was.

For weeks the talk went around the mines, saloons and streets that the local firemen would have a field day with a rival community. Bets were placed and firemen called upon to make speeches and pass the hat to raise prize money. The newspapers of each town helped work up the spirit of win-win to a fever pitch. Brother fought cousin over the merits of this team or that and when the big day arrived, crowds followed the band to the railroad station to the brassy blare of "Oh, Susanna," to greet the visitors with cheers and jeers and escort them to that level stretch south of town where those two ranchers fought that duel.

There were fire drills, pumping contests and boxing matches. Then came the hose cart and hose-laying races. In the wet test competition, the teams ran 500 feet to a water pipe, laying 200 feet of hose, connected it and got water. Good time for the event was 37 to 40 seconds. There was the dry test and then the final race for the big money. Teams ran 450 feet to water, laid 350 feet of hose, twice replacing lengths of hose with water shut off and then shooting a stream for distance. "May the best team win—and who wants to bet there ain't three people in town sober tonight!"

NANAIMO HOSE TEAM in Vancouver, British Columbia, ready to race Vancouver team.

FIRE DRILL CONTEST between crews of Northern Commercial Co., St. Michael, Alaska, 1908.

HOWARD HOOK AND LADDER CO., San Diego, California, on July 4, 1887.

(Above) TEST OF AHRENS ENGINE at courthouse in San Diego—1906. (Below) THE TIGERS
—Spokane's first fire department, 1885.

(Above) COMETS HOSE-LAYING TEAM of Spokane Falls defeated Seattle for State Championship at Corbin Park Race Track in 1884. (Below) Kamloops, British Columbia, fire brigade entry in inter-city reel races in early 1900s.

NOME FIRE DEPARTMENT on parade July 4, 1901.

EARLY STEAMER on First
South Street, Salt Lake City.

"Here Come the Horses..."

A first fascinating look at the fire-breathing monster they called a steamer must have made the stoutest heart of a volunteer fireman sink with dismay. It was true, then, he must have thought, the machine age is here and my years of loving toil are just about fond memories . . . "and look at that big beauty belch smoke! Bet she can pump a thousand gallons a minute and nobody working her but the stoker!"

Whether they realized it or not, the big steam-pumping engines spelled doom for the volunteer firemen. Fires were getting bigger and oftener with the growth of the towns, distances between engine house and fire longer — and how many men would it take to haul one of those big heavy steamer brutes with all those pipes and gauges? It was too bad to think human muscle which had always fought fires was now going down the drain, too bad to think how much money the steamers and hook and ladder wagons were going to cost. And who was going to furnish the horses and pay for their upkeep?

The answers were some time in coming and when they came the volunteer firemen had given way to paid professionals whose work was split between fire fighting and horse handling. For a while the smaller western towns manned their new steam rigs with volunteers, who, when an alarm was sounded, went dashing to the livery stable where a horse would be ready for use. Sometimes a town or private barn would loan a horse or two to the fire company if they could be spared from street cleaning or garbage hauling.

By this time, the bigger towns and cities had installed horses in the firehouses or in stables next door as part of the regular equipment. If the horses were kept in station stalls, harness was suspended over the wagon shaft by an automatic iron hanger. When the alarm sounded, springs released the stall doors or chains across stall openings, the horses sprang to action under their individual sets of harness, alert and quivering with

147

excitement as the driver leaped to his seat and pulled on the reins which dropped the harness. The house man snapped the special collars and automatic weights attached to small pulleys lifted the harness framework out of the way and—*clang, clang, clang,* the steamer lumbered out into the street. The stoker on the rear step had the coal fire going, needle already creeping up on the steam gauge, bystanders were gawking, small boys whooping and a pie-eyed Irishman yelling, "They're movin' hell! One load's gone by already!"

There were many rugged individualists among western volunteer firemen who "wouldn't be chambermaid to any damned nag," who could not abide thoughts of sharing their glory with horses. They knew in their stout hearts fires were started by humans to be put out by human strength and daring. Well, the conformists argued, there was still glory in the business, with service to town and humanity. These big powerful engines, they said, are here to stay and, mister, you'd better get on the bandwagon or your days of eating smoke are over. So the die-hards dropped out and in spite of the labor of cleaning the horses after a battle with the flames or putting in station house duty with stable sounds and odors, the compromisers began to like the idea of powerful apparatus pulled by powerful horses. They respected those willing, courageous, hard-working animals and grew to be fiercely proud of them. They were carefully curried and combed, hooves oiled and sometimes painted black. Some engine houses had a nightly ritual of bedding down the horses which became the darlings of the neighborhood, fascinating children and having men bring them lumps of sugar.

"Going like a fire horse" became part of the language and legends about fire horses part of the lore. When thirsty, one horse would release the lock on his stall door, walk to the sink and open the faucet with his teeth. One was an inveterate "hand shaker" and another got so impatient waiting for the house man to release the harness over his position, he would do it himself. Then there was the stubborn horse who refused to move if any fireman got on the hose wagon before he was hitched.

Experienced horses felt the importance and excitement of their work and responded eagerly to every task. Some seemed to be aware of the alarm bell strokes and could recognize the box numbers which they indicated. A highly drilled team could get apparatus rolling with incredible speed. It was not unusual for equipment to be out of the station and on the street eighteen seconds after the alarm.

ENGINE NO. 1 of Seattle Volunteer Fire Department, photographed July 23, 1883. Nozzleman Joe Keppler stands at left. Holding Lizzie McDonald is Engineer Will Perry. First by rear wheel is Suctionman Oscar Kreig, behind him Stoker John Storm. Bystander at right with boys is Al Cutler.

(Above) HORSES FOR HEAVY HAULING. Spokane Steamer No. 4 (Below) Early hose reel rig in Spokane using lighter horses.

(Above) TERRIER MASCOT rides with firemen on Nome hose wagon. (Right) Three-horse team gallops to Seattle fire in 1909. Photo taken at 4th near Thomas. (Below, left to right) Nanaimo, British Columbia, steamer in 1896; Hamilton Engine Co. No. 2, San Diego, California, 1889; First fire horses in Canon City, Colorado in 1909.

ENGINE #4 - 1909

VIRGINIA M. TUTT BRANCH
2002 Miami Street
South Bend, Indiana 46613

(Above) SEATTLE STEAMER,
1907. (Below) Nome, Alaska,
fire crew in early 1900s.

(Opposite top) HELENA, Montana, fire department about 1880
a n d (bottom) Rainier Valley
(Seattle) hose reel rig.

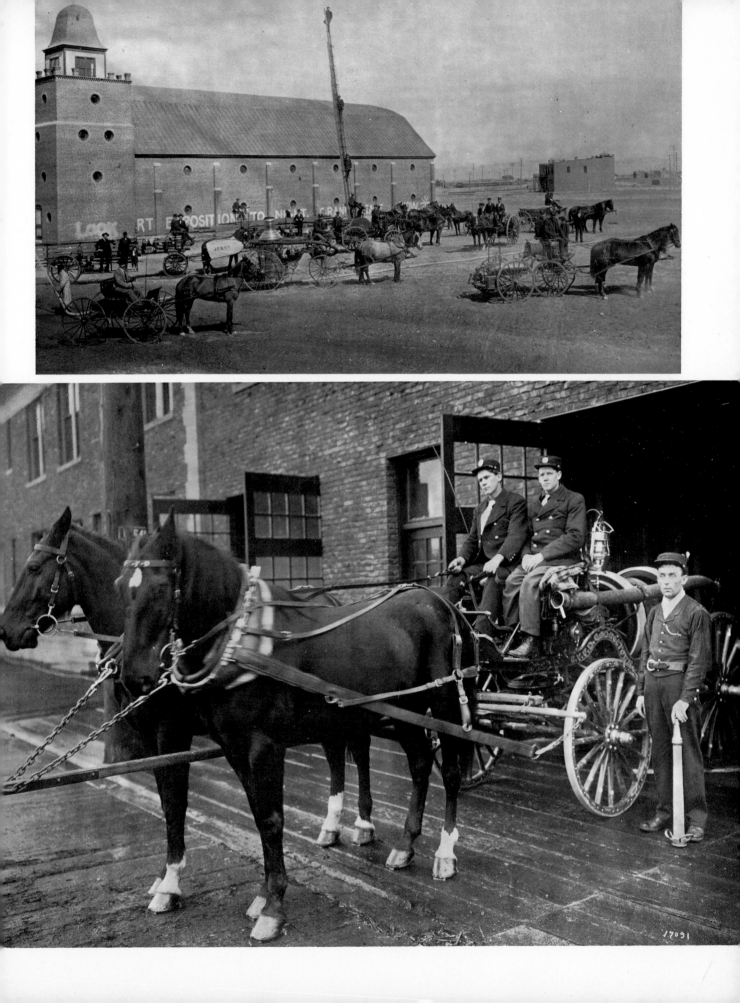

Tom

Johnny

Joe

Judy

Bill

Dick

Dock

Frank

Joe

Dimple

Charlie

Chuck

Jerry

Engine-No 1 – Purchased by City of Se

Pat

Ned

Spike

Replaced by Motor-1924.

Don

Mike

King

Dan

Bob

Duke

Cap

GOODBYE DON, DIMPLE and all the other Seattle fire horses. All were named, all were pampered, all were relegated to menial tasks w h e n gasoline trucks replaced them in 1924. In center oval is Engine No. 1 purchased by City of Seattle in 1889.

(Above) SEATTLE HOSE WAGON: driver, A. P. Gough, on step, Ray Milton. (Left) How much horse power in six dogs? Chemical fire engine drawn by sled dogs in Dawson, Yukon Territory.

(Bottom, left to right) DENVER HOSE CART; Canon City, Colorado, fire wagon in 1909; Highland Hose Co. No. 1, Denver, 1901.

(Above) READY FOR AN ALARM — Seattle Co. 9 in 1916. (Below, center) 85-foot American La France aerial ladder at Seattle Fire Dept. headquarters, 2nd and Main, 1906. (Bottom) Champion water tower in Seattle, 1905.

VISITING FIREMEN. Gard Kellogg, chief of Seattle Fire Dept., entertaining David Campbell,
chief of Portland Fire Dept., with other visitors and chiefs aboard fireboat *Snoqualmie* in early 1900s.

GRAND TRUNK DOCK

GRAND TRUNK DOCK CAS-
UALTY. Injured man being
taken from burning dock in Seat-
tle, 1914. (Left) Seattle Fire
Department headquarters at 3rd
South and Main, 1904.

FULL HEAD OF STEAM. Spokane engine throws two jets of water as engineer studies
column of black smoke. Stoker at left is ready to empty another sack of coal in the fuel bay.

(Above) MT. VERNON NO. 1, dated 1880, was used in Sonoma County, California.   (Below) 1905 steamer in San Diego, California, 1905.

SAN DIEGO No. 1—early steamer used about time of Standard Oil Co. tank fire, Oct. 5, 1913, shown below.

FLAMES ROAR from top story of Mutual Life Insurance building at California and Sansome Streets in San Francisco 1906 earthquake and fire as financial district burns. Across street at right Fireman's Fund building is next to go. Firemen stand helpless, limp hoses connected to hydrants that bring no water, mains throughout city broken by quake.

ASTORIA FIRE DEC. 8. 1922

Frank Woodfield

OREGON *40 blocks in Astoria burned Dec. 8, 1922*

(Above) EARLY IN MORNING Astoria, Oregon, fire sprang up in various parts of business district which was built on creosoted piling over tide flats.

(Below) WATERFRONT did not burn. Pumpers on docks were isolated when flames were carried into business area away from Columbia River shown in background.

Trench Photo #21 Commercial St. Looking East Astoria Ore. Dec 1922.

NO. 3 ASTORIA Fire Department in 1902. Firemen left to right are: Al Leinenweber, Charles Olson, Roxey Graham, Ole Gunderson, Walter Peterson, Ted Sutton, Fire Chief Stockton.

(Above) GUARD PATROLS devastated area in Astoria, Oregon, after December 1922 fire.

(Right) BUILDINGS on waterfront suffered little damage. Washington shore shown in background across Columbia River.

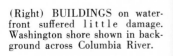

Fire Fighting Started Early in Salem

They had no hooks and no ladders but they had to do something. The new $27,000 territorial statehouse had just burned down and the town knew it had to have fire protection. So during the closing days of 1855, Salem's Alert Hook and Ladder Co. was formed. In ten years the Webfoot Co. No. 1 came into being and was later named Capital Engine Co. No. 1, then came Tiger Co. No. 2 and in 1889, Salem Engine Co. No. 3.

The capital city blazed furiously and frequently in the '60s, wrote Ben Maxwell in the Salem *Capital Journal*. One fire started in "Patcheye" Burns' Crystal Saloon on May 10, 1863 and wiped out a few blocks of frame shacks. The next year the Mansion House was destroyed with every fire trap on the south side of State Street between Liberty and High. The Belvidere Saloon and frowsy buildings near it were burned out in 1865; Capital House bar-room and adjacent buildings in 1869.

Two unforgettable fires, says Maxwell, occurred in the 1880s. The pioneer Bennett House, which had deteriorated into a Chinese dive, went up in smoke January 14, 1887, taking three opium smokers with it.

In 1893 the days of the Salem volunteer firemen came to an end with the hiring of professional fire fighters. Then in 1900, the city having a population of 4,253, the fire department could boast of a La France steam pumper, smaller Silsby engine, light-running hose truck and two powerful teams of horses.

(Above) EARLY FIRE CHIEF in Salem, Oregon. (Right) Hunneman pumper used by Webfoot No. 1 in Salem starting May 29, 1865, now treasured relic in Salem Fire Dept., E. Salem Station. (Opposite, top) Salem volunteer fire crew in 1886.

(Above) SALEM, OREGON, PRIDE AND JOY was La France steamer, parade winner in 1896. Stuffed fox above pressure gauge was symbol of crew's speed and alacrity. City had paid department at this time and 4 companies — Capital Engine Co. No. 1; Tiger Engine Co. No. 2 and Salem Engine Co. No. 3. (Below) Volunteer crew in 1886 teaming up for hose cart race.

(Right) GRANITE, OREGON, fire hall as it appeared in 1961. (Below) Fire hall at Antelope, Wasco County, Oregon, with fire bell on trellis at right of building.

FIREMEN'S PARADE and Tournament on Commercial Street, Salem, Oregon, in mid-1880s.

VIRGINIA CITY pioneer fire-house—Divide Hose Co. No. 2.

Bunk Rooms
and Brass Poles

The life of a professional fireman in the early days was ninety percent fighting, not fires but boredom. Not for the volunteer firemen, of course. Most of them had jobs and gave only extra time to run to fires and maybe a day a week for clean-up work in the firehouse. But the men who spent ten or twelve hours every day or night with one ear on the alarm bell, the other on buzzing flies or philosophy from a cane-bottomed chair, — they were the ones who put in time the hard way.

You bet there was work to do in the station and, when there wasn't, men with initiative had study courses and hobbies to pursue. The apparatus was in constant need of cleaning, the brass always needed polishing. After a run back from a fire the steamer, chemical wagon or hook and ladder were washed down and the painted surfaces wiped dry. If hose had been used, it was laid out to dry. There were always repairs to be made to engines and machinery, maintenance work inside and out. Horses had to be cared for. And there was always the daily fire drill to keep men alert and try to clip another minute off the time between alarm and getaway.

The time of some firemen was taken up by charity work for they were in a glamorous profession and their presence at meetings and socials added color and prestige to the occasion. There were athletic contests, baseball games, parades, all of which required training and preparation. Public officials were fond of calling on the more articulate firemen to head this or that committee or to attend ribbon-cutting ceremonies or dedication of new community buildings.

And every fire station in the glory days must have its bunkroom and kitchen. A full crew was required ready and able to jump to the rigs at the first *clang* of the alarm bell, so meals and sleep must be subject to that call. Work was usually arranged so that only a few men on duty would be sleeping or eating at the same time.

The bunkroom was usually on the second floor, above the apparatus and horses, with food storage and perhaps pool or card tables on the floor above, to which hay for the horses was hoisted by block-and-tackle at the rear. The bunkroom contained little but cots with a circular hole in the floor centered by the brass pole. When the men went to bed, their suspendered pants were draped over their boots by the side of the cot. Responding to the alarm required little more motion than a leap from cot to clothes, a quick flip of the galluses over the shoulder, another jump to the brass pole and a fast slide to the ground floor where the apparatus might already be in motion.

The men on watch through the long night hours played cards, read newspapers and listened to each other expound on subjects covered hundreds of earlier times. The afternoons passed somewhat quicker with visitors to see the fire horses or the new red steamer and maybe the lady in the house across the street brought over a cake or sack of apples. And boys always had to be watched to see that they did not sneak under the chains across the doorways and hide somewhere in the shadows.

Every firehouse worth its keep had a mascot or pet of some kind. Traditionally it was a dog, Dalmatian preferred, who would run to the fire ahead of the horses to clear the street, or ride to it on the apparatus and stand guard, allowing no one but firemen near it. Other dogs would stay in the stations while men and equipment were out to see that no one entered. There are tales told of cats trained to slide down the brass poles, of monkeys who rode on the backs of the horses, but dogs were considered the most useful mascot, the most constant members of every fire crew.

FIRE STATION IN NOME, Alaska, housing bell and hose reel, about 1902.

(Above) WHITE SULPHUR SPRINGS, Montana, fire department. (Below) Museum display in Great Falls, Montana, showing apparatus once used in Anaconda. At first sound of alarm, horses ran under harness, driver jumped to seat and released trigger which dropped collars and harness, weights pulling rigging up out of way.

(Below) TUOLUMNE, California, Engine House No. 1 during gold rush days.

(Above) SAN FRANCISCO. Empire Engine Co. No. 1, Sacramento Street between Kearny and Grant, old St. Mary's church in background. Was organized after first great fire on June 4, 1850 with D. C. Broderick as first foreman. In 1851, it had target company with 125 muskets. Apparatus was New York side-lever engine.

(Right) SAN FRANCISCO. Knickerbocker Engine Co. No. 5 on Sacramento Street between Sansome and Leidesdorff. Organized in 1850, first location destroyed by fire Nov. 9, 1852. Equipment was mahogany piano box engine made by Smith at cost of $3,250. Later patron was Lillie Hitchcock Coit who gave Coit Tower to city.

(Above) SAN FRANCISCO. Members of Columbia Engine Co. No. 11, organized Oct. 25, 1852 and disbanded Dec. 2, 1866. (Opposite) Columbia Co.'s house on north side of Bush St. between Kearny and Grant. Engine is Van Ness piano box with running gear.

(Left) SAN FRANCISCO. St. Francis Hook and Ladder Co. in 1856, on Dupont Street between Clay and Sacramento. Organized in June 1850.

(Above) SAN FRANCISCO.
Eureka Engine Co. at corner of
Mason and Sutter Streets in 1862.

(Right) SALT LAKE CITY fire
department.

SAN DIEGO Fire Station No. 1 between Market and Island Streets about 1895. Hook and ladder rig was designed by A. B. Cairnes who was chief 1889-1905.

(Above) SALT LAKE CITY Fire Station No. 2 showing part of last roll call of Mormon Volunteer Fire Department on Dec. 31, 1889.

(Right) SALT LAKE CITY Fire Department in front of City Hall. (Below) Rossland, British Columbia, fire hall and equipment in 1910.

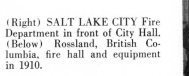

NELSON, BRITISH COLUMBIA, fire hall.

FIRST MOTOR TRUCKS in Kamloops, British Columbia, 1911.

Trucks Get There Faster

The fire horse and very few firemen saw any menace in the mechanical marvels that were tearing up the dusty roads at 20 miles an hour in the early 1900s. With intuition, they might have seen visions of self-propelled contraptions being driven by daredevils but who was crazy enough to predict they would eventually replace the horse? *Scribner's Magazine* was. In a 1902 issue a writer said is was very probable the days of the fire horse were numbered, that either electricity or steam was likely to be the force to do it.

Then in a few years trucks were coming out in all shapes and sizes, using all kinds of fuel including coal and, of all things, gasoline. Some of the models were fire trucks, some horse-drawn steamers converted into what were now called automobiles. Then a two-wheeled engine was developed to haul the old equipment and by 1910 a wide and grotesque variety of fire trucks was making a bid for municipal purses. In a few more years engine companies began to buy gasoline driven rigs that used the same motor for driving and pumping. Alameda, California, had one of the first ones. They broke down often, the skeptical public laughed and most fire chiefs kept some horses to fall back on.

But by 1920 trucks were getting to the fires first and even the fire house doubters could see horses walking out the back doors instead of running out the front, the stables being cleaned for the last time. In another few years the transition was about over. Fire trucks were efficient, fast and handsome and so was the new breed of fireman who scorned the tears of old-timers as they lost their four-footed friends. The fire house dog was bewildered and skulked behind the proud horses as they were led to farms and uncertain futures but the general melancholy was short lived. The industrial revolution had set in and adherents of the new day welcomed it with sirens screaming as history was made with new speed records on every fire run.

(Left) THE GONG CLANGS AT MIDNIGHT. Seattle fire truck No. 1 going out on call on July 31, 1916.

(Opposite, bottom) CHEMICAL ENGINE. Seattle Fire Department, 1910.

(Below) FIRE TRUCKS IN SNOW. Kamloops, British Columbia.

SEAGRAVE FIRE TRUCK at explosion in Italian National Macaroni Co. plant, National City, California, on Sept. 1, 1912.

INDEX

ABERDEEN *BULLETIN* 140
Aberdeen Livery and Transfer Co. 138
Aberdeen, Wash. 138-140
Adler and Berry Saloon 88
Ahrens Engine 144
Alameda, Calif. 145
Alaska 77, 78
Alaska Building 117
Alder, Douglas D. 169
Alderson, Frank 48
Alert Hook and Ladder Co. 168
Alexander, R. H. 95
American-La France Aerial Ladder 158
Anaconda, Mont. 175
Ancon 118
Anderson and Middleton Mill 140
Angel, Myron 48
Annals of San Francisco 56-61, 100
Anstie, Chief 139, 140
Antelope, Ore. 171
Arcade Block 117
Arctic Hotel 138, 140
Arlington Hotel 114, 133
Armory Hall 121
Armstrong, B.C. 97
Astoria, Ore. 55, 165-167

BABCOCK HOOK AND LADDER CO.
   38
Back, John E. 105
Baer, Harry 131
Baer, Louis 131
Bagley, Clarence B. 105, 106, 112, 113
Baillargeon and Co. 118
Baldwin Hotel 59
Bank of British Columbia 91
Bank of British North America 77
Bank of Commerce 83, 118
Barkerville, B. C. 18, 88, 90
Barkley Store, A. W. 139
Barnett's Brick Block 51
Barrett, Patrick 33
Beaton, Welford 121
Beck, Mrs. John 51
Bell and Burke 51
Bellingham, Wash. 105
Belvidere Saloon 168
Bennett House 168
Beshoar, Camp 42
Best, John 38
Bigelow's Opera House 48
Bingham Canyon, Utah 72
Black Hawk, Colo. 38
"Black Hole of Ludlow" 47
Bon Accord 91
Boswell and Co. 38
Boulder *News* 38
Boultbee, J. 95
Bowes, Jim 138
Boyd, W. P. 118

Boyd's Photograph Gallery 114
Brackman and Ker Dock 91
Broderick, D. C. 176
Broderick No. 1 101
Brown, Amos 114
Brown, Fireman 11
Bundy, George E. 105, 109, 123
Burke Block 112
Burns, "Patch Eye" 168
Burns and Co. 86
Butler Hotel 117

CAIRNES, A. B. 182
Campbell, Chief David 159
Campbell, Scotty 138, 139
Canadian Pacific Navigation 91
Canadian Pacific Railway 82, 96
Canon City, Colo. 19, 150, 157
Capital Engine Co. No. 1 170
"Carey Castle" 98
Carey, G. H. 98
Cariboo Sentinel 88
Carson City, Nev. 49, 50, 51
Carson Engine 100
Central City, Colo. 38, 39
Central Dance Hall 23
Central School 139
Champion Water Tower 158
Charot's Restaurant 38
Chicago, Ill. 123
Chillberg and Co. 118
Circle City, Alaska 14
City That Made Itself, The 121
Clark, Bob 82
Cleary, Chester 125
Coeur d'Alenes 128
Cohn, Jacob 49
Coit, Lillie Hitchcock 177
Collier, Samuel 121
Collins House 117
Collins, Chief Josiah 106, 123
Colman Block 112, 114
Colonial Block 112
Colorado 22-47
Colorado and Southern Railroad 40
Colorado City, Colo. 24
Colorado National Guard 40, 41
Colorado Springs, Colo. 24
Columbia Engine Co. No. 11 178
Columbia River 167
Comets Hose Laying Team 145
Commercial Bakery 140
Commercial Hotel 130
Commercial Mill 109, 112, 114
Concert Hall 38
Conner, Mrs. Emily 50
Consolidated Mercur Mines 69
Consolidated Virginia Mine 50
Corbin Park Race Track 145
Cornish Hall 33

Cosmopolis, Wash. 139, 140
Cranbrook, B. C. 82
Crawford and Conover 110
Crawford's Drug Store 38
Crescent Hotel 140
Cripple Creek, Colo. 22-30
Crocker Building, H. S. 59
Crystal Saloon 168
Curtis, J. H. 74
Curtis, Rev. Dr. 74
Cutler, Al 148

DABNEY, R. T. 140
Daly City, Calif. 101
Davis, Griffith 12
Davis, W. D. 50
Dawson, Y. T. 76, 77, 157
Dean, Mrs. Ed 50
Denny Home 125
Denver, Colo. 17, 38, 157
Denver *Republican* 31
Depot Hotel 51
Devine, Chief James 20
Devine, John 50
Divide Hose Co. No. 2 173
Dobson House 33
Douglas Building 49
Downey, Fireman 11
Durant, R. L. 118
Durham, N. W. 128
Duwamish 126, 127

EAGLE BUILDING 129
Edgar 91
Egan's Hall 33
Elk Valley Lumber Co. 80
Elks Building 140
Ellis Brothers 74
Ellis, G. S. 74
Empire Engine Co. 101, 176
Esmeralda County, Nev. 54
Eureka Engine Co. 181
Eureka *Leader* 49
Eureka, Nev. 48, 49
Eureka *Sentinel* 49

FALLNER, CHARLES 51
Fashion Saloon 138
Federal Building 121
Federal Commission on Industrial
   Relations 42
Fernie, B. C. 80-84
Fernie-Fort Steele Brewery 80
Ferry, E. P. 121
Fireman's Fund Insurance Co. 101, 164
Fireman's Hall 140
Fireman's Herald 100
First National Bank 133
First Regiment, N.G.W. 119
Fitzpatrick, James 151
Fleetwood 118

Flood, Harry 131
Foley-Rickard Black 49
Forbes Tent Colony 44
Fountain Head Restaurant 50
Frankfort Block 129, 131
Freas and Raynolds 38
Frye's Opera House 109, 112
Furth, Jacob 121
Furth, Mayor 128

GEORGETOWN, COLO. 31, 141
Gessler, Fred 38
"Ghost of Mercur" 69
Gladys 91
Gleason, Fireman 11
Gold Coin Mine 37
Golden, Colo. 38
Golden Gate Mill 70
Goldfield, Nev. 48, 54
Goldstein, Charles 118
Gordon Hardware 118
Gough, A. P. 157
Gould Pumper 105
Graham, Roxey 166
Grand Trunk Dock Title page, 125, 126, 160
Granite, Ore. 171
Granite Building 129
Grant, Rev. Hugh
Great Falls, Mont. 175
Great Northern Railway 80, 82
Gunderson, Ole 166
Guthrie, Chief D. 86
Gylfe, Alex 138

HAINES, COL. J. C. 119
Hall and Hagedorn 74
Hamilton Engine Co. 150
Hanford, Judge Cornelius 121
Hanson, Albert 118
Harbor Queen 140
Harris and Greenus 112
Hart Hook and Ladder Co. 19
Hastings Hill 94, 95, 96
Havre, Mont. 14
Heilbron, George H. 121
Helena, Mont. 14, 17, 19, 54, 73-75, 152
Helena *Daily Herald* 74
Helena *Gazette* 74
Hershberg and Co. 118
Heuse, J. H. 38
Highland Boy Mine 72
Highland Hose Co. No. 1 157
Hillhouse, A. M. 49
Hinckley Block 114
History of the City of Spokane 128
History of Nevada 48
History of Seattle 105, 113
Hogan, Grandmother 51
Holyoke Block 114
"Hometown Scrapbook" 138
Hooligan Hill 53
Hoquiam, Wash. 139, 140
Hosmer, B. C. 80
Hotel Lincoln 108
Howard Engine Co. 20
Howard Hook and Ladder Co. 143
Hudson's Bay Co. 88
Hunneman Pumper 168
Hunneman, William C. 100
Hutching's Magazine 10
Hyde Block 129

INTERNATIONAL HOTEL 49, 86
Italian National Macaroni Co. 188
Irvine, Robert 51

JACKSON HOUSE 48
Jennings and Boise Saloon 33
Jimtown, Colo. 31
Jones, Superintendent 128, 131
Johnson, C. G. 95
Johnson, Mrs. Lena 51
Johnstown Flood 121

KAMLOOPS, B.C. 145, 185, 187
KBKW Station 138
Kellogg, Gardner 106, 118, 123, 159
Kelowna, B.C. 101
Kenny Building 112
Kenyon Block 112
Keppler, Joe 147
Kincaid, Gov. 49
Kingsgate, B. C. 82
Knapp, Burrell and Co. 114
Knickerbocker Engine Co. No. 1 177
Knox, Charles 50
Koehler, Chief 139, 140
Kreig, Oscar 147

LA FRANCE PUMPER 168, 170
LaFayette Hook and Ladder Co. 54
Lapham, Mayor Roger D. 101
Larkin, Nick 138
Lautenschlager's Saloon 49
Leary, John 121
Leinenweber, Al 166
Lewis, J. R. 121
Logan, William 40
Lonkey and Smith Lumber Yard 50
Low, Billy 50
Ludlow, Colo. 40-47
Ludlow Tent Colony 40-47
Lynch Saloon, Patrick 50
Lytton Hotel 91

McDONALD, JACK 82, 123
McDonald, Lizzie 147
McGough, Jim 105
McInnes Saloon 88
McInnes, T. R. E. 98
McKinney, E. C. 51
McLoughlin and Bridges 112
McLoughlin and Root Building 50

MacINTOSH, ANGUS 121
Mack Building 138, 139
Maddocks, M. R. 114
Maley, Les 138
Mandel, Ben 50
"Mankiller" 100
Mansion House 168
Mason, Allen C. 121
Masonic Hall 48, 51
Maxwell, Ben 168
Meiggs Wharf 17
Merchants National Bank 118, 121
Mercer, Utah 69-71
Merriwether Engine 119
Methodist Church 73, 74
Methodist Episcopal Church 49
Mexico 118
Midland Ticket Office 22

Miller, Carl 73
Milton, Ray 157
Mock, Mr. 48
Montana Lumber Yard 126
Montesano, Wash. 140
Moore Land Co. 121
Moran, Mayor Robert 112, 119, 121
Moran's Machine Shop 117
Mormon Volunteer Fire Department 183
Mount Vernon No. 1 162
Murphy, Bill 140
Music Hall 50
Mutual Life Insurance Co. 164

NANAIMO, B.C. 12, 17, 142, 150
National Archives 42
National City, Calif. 188
Nelson, B. C. 79, 184
Nevada State Flouring Mills 51
New Westminster, B.C. 91-93
New Westminster *Columbian* 91
New York Engine 176
Nome, Alaska 77-78, 146, 150, 152, 174
"North Fork Fire Department" 141
"North Fork News Nugget" 141
North Pacific Hotel 74
Northern Commercial Co. 143
Northern Pacific Railroad 117, 128, 129, 131, 134, 135
Northwestern Cracker Co. 114

OCCIDENTAL HOTEL 117, 118
Odd Fellows Hall 49
Olson, Charles 166
Olympia, Wash. 105, 121
Ophir Mine 50

PACIFIC COAST CO. 118
Pacific Hotel 129
Palace Drug Store 22
Palace Restaurant 112
Paxton's Bank 48, 49
Perry's Saloon 48, 49
Perry, Will 147
Peterson, Walter 166
Pfund, Emil 138
Phoenix Stamp Works 135
Pioche *Journal* 53
Pioche, Nev. 52
Pioche *Record* 53
Pioneer Block 117
Pioneer Place 115
Poncin Block 117
Pontius Block 105, 106, 109
Poplin Store 49
Port Townsend, Wash. 105
Portland Hotel 24
Portland, Ore. 105, 112, 118
Potter, T. J. 119
Preble Building 69
Prefontaine, Father 117
Preston Aerial Truck 105
Puget Sound National Bank 115
Pumphrey and Co. 118

RAILROAD HOUSE 51
Rainier Valley, Wash. 99, 152
Rawhide, Nev. 53
Register Building 38
Reinig Building 112
Reno, *Journal* 51
Reno, Nev. 49, 50, 51

Revelstoke, B. C. 13
Revere, Paul 100
Rialto Building 121
Riverside Hotel 49
Roche, G. W. 131
Robert Dunsmuir 95
Rocky Mountain News 38, 40
Rogers, Capt. 95
Rolfe, Charles 139
Rosenfeld, Smith Co. 125
Rossland, B.C. 86, 87, 183
Royal City Planing Mills 94

SACRAMENTO ENGINE 99, 102
St. Charles Hotel 117
St. Francis Hook and Ladder Co. 180
St. Michaels, Alaska 143
St. Paul, Minn 123
Salem Capital-Journal 168
Salem Engine Co. No. 3 168, 170
Salem, Ore. 168-170, 172
Salt Lake City, Utah 15, 20, 147, 181, 183
San Diego, Calif. 19, 143, 144, 150, 162, 163, 182
San Francisco, Calif. 20, 55-67, 101, 121, 164, 176, 177, 178, 179, 180, 181
San Francisco Store 112, 117
Schaffer, George 51
Schneider's Drug Store 49
Schwabacher's Wholesale House 118
Schweden, J. H. 38
Scott's Saloon 88
Scribner's Magazine 185
Seagrave Fire Truck 188
Seattle Chronicle 134
Seattle Electric Light Co. 114
Seattle Hardware Co. 118
Seattle Morning Journal 119
Seattle Post-Intelligencer 107, 119
Seattle Times 114
Seattle, Wash. Title page, 20, 99, 103, 104-127, 140, 145, 148, 150, 152, 154-5, 157, 158, 159, 160, 187
Seattle Water C. 119
Seller and Sauer 38
Siegel, A. W. 135
Silsby Engine 118, 168
Silver Plume, Colo. 21, 32
Silver Plume Coloradoan 33

Sinclair and Western Fisheries 91
Skid Road 112
S, L and E. Depot 113
Smith, J. P. 50
Snohomish, Wash. 105
Snoqualmie 159
Snyder, William 42
Snyder's Bakery 38
Sonoma County, Calif. 162
Soule, Frank 56, 100
Southwestern Mine 47
Squire, Watson C. 121
"Squirrel Tails" 100
Spokane Falls Review 128, 132
Spokane Falls, Wash. 11, 13, 17, 82, 128-137, 145, 149, 161
Spokane Furniture Co. 136
Standard Oil Co. 163
Star Hook and Ladder Co. 33, 141
Starr Block 117
Staver and Walker 114
Stewart and Holmes 118
Stockton, Chief 166
Storm, John 148
Sutton, Ted 166
Swift, S. T. 51

TABOR HOSE CO. 17
Tacoma Relief Bureau 121, 125
Tacoma, Wash. 105, 112, 117, 117, 119, 121, 140
Taylor Block 74
Teller House 38
Tiger Co. No. 2 168, 170
Tikas, Louis 41, 42
Thatcher, Stanley and Co. 38
Thayer, Ephriam 100
Thompson and West 48
Thomson, Rev. 95
Toklas and Kaufman Store 140
Toklas-Singerman's 117, 118
Trail, B.C. 86
Treen, L. A. 118
Trinidad, Colo. 40
Trinity Church 117
Truckee, Ariz. 51
Tull Building 129
Tuolumne, Calif. 176
Tutt and Penrose Block 28, 30
Tuttle, Mayor "Bill" 80, 81, 82

UNION BLOCK 112, 117
United Mine Workers or America 40, 42, 82
Utah Historical Quarterly 69

VAN BOKKELEN, MAJOR GENERAL 50
Van Ness Engine 178
Vancouver, B. C. 91, 94-96, 142
Vancouver Weekly Herald 94
Vanina and Co. 49
Victor, Colo. 24, 35-37
Victoria, B.C. 98, 105, 112, 119
Virginia City, Nev. 18, 50, 51, 103, 121, 173

WCTU 140
Wadsworth, Nev. 51
Walker's Resort For Gentlemen 138
Walsenburg, Colo. 40
Washington Iron Works 118
Waterfall, William 69
Watson, Acting Fire Chief 91
Weatherwax, Ben 138
Webfoot No. 1 168
Weill, I. 88
Weir Theater 140
Wells Fargo Co. 38
West and Slade Mill 140
West, Mayor 140
Western Hotel 50
Western Mills 105
Western Union Telegraph 48, 137
Westinghouse Engine 103
Whicher Machinery Exchange 139
White Building 114
White Sulphur Springs, Mont. 175
Whitlach Block 74
Williams Creek, B. C. 18
Winnipeg, Man. 82
Wishkah River 139, 140
Wolfe, George 140
Womack, Bob 24
Worth, William E. 101
Wychoff House 117

YALE, B. C. 85, 101
YMCA 91
Yesler, Henry 123
Yesler-Leary Block 117
Yesler Sawmill 115

PHOTO CREDITS

Frontispiece, Seattle Fire Department Collection

Page 10, Provincial Archives, Victoria, B.C.

Page 11, Eastern Washington State Historical Society, Spokane

Page 12, Provincial Archives, Victoria, B.C.

Page 13 top, Provincial Archives, Victoria, B.C.; bottom, Eastern Washington State Historical Society

Page 14, top and bottom, Montana Historical Society

Page 15 center, University of Washington Special Collections; top, right and bottom, Utah State Historical Society

Page 16 top, Bancroft Library, University of California; bottom, left, State Historical Society of Colorado; center, Eastern Washington State Historical Society

Page 17 top, Montana Historical Society; bottom, right, Provincial Archives, Victoria, B.C.

Page 18 top, Bancroft Library, University of California; bottom, Provincial Archives, Victoria, B.C.

Page 19 both State Historical Society of Colorado

Page 20 top, Title Ins. and Trust Co., San Diego; bottom, left, Seattle Fire Dept. Collection

Page 21 top, State Historical Society of Colorado; bottom, center, Utah State Historical Society; bottom, right, Bancroft Library, University of California

Page 22 top, Denver Western Library; bottom, State Historical Society of Colorado

Page 23 Denver Western Library

Pages 24-25 and 26, State Historical Society of Colorado

Page 27 top, Denver Western Library; bottom, State Historical Society of Colorado

Pages 28-29 and 30, Denver Western Library

Page 31, State Historical Society of Colorado

Page 32, Denver Western Library

Pages 34-35, 36-37, 39, 40-47 State Historical Society of Colorado

Pages 48-49, 52-53 Nevada Historical Society

Page 54 top, Montana Historical Society; bottom, Nevada Historical Society

Page 55, Clatsop Co. (Ore.) Historical Society

Page 56 and 59, Bancroft Library, University of California

Page 63 top, Calif. Palace of Legion of Honor; bottom, Wells Fargo History Room

Page 64 top and center, Calif. Palace of Legion of Honor; bottom, Bancroft Library, University of California

Page 65 top right and bottom, Bancroft Library, University of California

Pages 66-67 top center, Bancroft Library, University of California; all others, Calif. Palace of Legion of Honor

Pages 68-72 Utah State Historical Society

Pages 73 and 75, Montana Historical Society

Pages 76 and 77, Bancroft Library, University of California

Page 78, University of Washington Special Collections

Pages 79-98, Provincial Archives, Victoria, B.C.

Page 99, Washington State Historical Society

Page 101, Fireman's Fund Insurance Co., S.F.

Page 102, University of Washington Special Collections

Page 103 top, Bancroft Library, University of California; bottom, Seattle Fire Department Collection

Page 104, Washington State Historical Society

Page 106, University of Washington Special Collections

Pages 107-109, Seattle Fire Department Collection

Pages 110-120, University of Washington Special Collections

Page 122, Seattle Fire Department Collection

Pages 123-127, University of Washington Special Collections

Pages 128-137, Eastern Washington State Historical Society

Page 138 and 139, Jones Studio, Aberdeen

Page 141, State Historical Society of Colorado

Page 142, Provincial Archives, Victoria, B.C.

Page 143 top, Bancroft Library, University of California; bottom, Title Ins. and Trust Co., San Diego

Page 144 top, Title Ins. and Trust Co., San Diego; bottom, Eastern Washington State Historical Society

Page 145 top, Eastern Washington State Historical Society; bottom, Provincial Archives, Victoria, B.C.

Page 146, University of Washington Special Collections

Pages 147 and 148, Seattle Fire Department Collection

Page 149, Eastern Washington State Historical Society

Page 150 top, left, Bancroft Library, University of California; bottom, left, Provincial Archives, Victoria, B.C.; center, Title Ins. and Trust Co., San Diego

Page 151 top, Seattle Fire Department Collection

Page 152 top, University of Washington Special Collections; bottom, Bancroft Library, University of California

Page 153 top, Montana Historical Society; bottom, Washington State Historical Society

Pages 154-5, Seattle Fire Department Collection

Page 156 top, University of Washington Special Collections; bottom, left, State Historical Society of Colorado

Page 157 top right, Seattle Fire Department Collection; bottom center and right, State Historical Society of Colorado

Pages 158-160, Seattle Fire Department Collection

Page 161, Eastern Washington State Historical Society

Page 162 top, Bancroft Library, University of California; bottom, Title Ins. and Trust Co., San Diego

Page 163 Title Ins. and Trust Co., San Diego

Page 164, Fireman's Fund Insurance Co., S.F.

Pages 165 and 166-7. Clatsop Co. (Ore.) Historical Society

Page 168 left, Oregon State Library

Page 169 top, Oregon State Library; bottom, Ben Maxwell, Salem

Page 170 top, Ben Maxwell, Salem; bottom, Oregon State Library

Pages 171 and 172, Ben Maxwell, Salem

Pages 173 and 174, Bancroft Library, University of California

Page 175, Montana Historical Society

Page 176, Bancroft Library, University of California

Pages 177, 178, 179, 180 and 181, Bancroft Library, Hill Collection, University of California

Page 181 bottom, Utah State Historical Society

Page 182, Title Ins. and Trust Co., San Diego

Page 183 top and center, Utah State Historical Society; bottom, Provincial Archives, Victoria, B.C.

Pages 184 and 185, Provincial Archives, Victoria, B.C.

Page 186, Seattle Fire Department Collection

Page 187 bottom, Provincial Archives, Victoria, B.C.

Page 188, Bancroft Library, University of California

Page 192, Provincial Archives, Victoria, B.C.

VIRGINIA M. TUTT BRANCH
2002 Miami Street
South Bend, Indiana 46613

OCT 1 - 1980

WITHDRAWN